DEPENDENCE
in the Life of Christ

ENCOURAGEMENT AND CHALLENGE
TO TRUE DISCIPLESHIP

123 meditations for devotional times

Jan Philip Svetlik

DEPENDENCE
in the Life of Christ

ENCOURAGEMENT AND CHALLENGE
TO TRUE DISCIPLESHIP

123 meditations for devotional times

Jan Philip Svetlik

The Bereans Publishing Ltd.
38 Mountain Road
Kilkeel, Co. Down
BT34 4BB
United Kingdom
info@the-bereans.com
www.the-bereans.com

Believer's Bookshelf Canada Inc.
5205 Regional Rd #81, Unit # 3
Beamsville, Ontario
L0R1B3
Canada
orders@bbcan.org
www.believersbookshelf.ca

ISBN: 978-1-913232-44-3
All Rights Reserved
Copyright: © The Bereans Publishing Ltd.
Second edition 2021

The Bereans Publishing Ltd.
United Kingdom
info@the-bereans.com, www.the-bereans.com

and

Believers Bookshelf Canada Inc.
Canada
orders@bbcan.org, www.believersbookshelf.ca

Original German publication:
Ernst-Paulus Verlag
Erfurter Straße 4
67433 Neustadt
Germany
info@epvneustadt.de

Cover design: David Lehnhardt

Printed in Germany

Table of contents

Opening Remarks

It's always a special blessing to reflect on the life of the Lord Jesus. His name is Wonderful—and so was His whole life here on earth. He is so unfathomably great that He told His disciples, *"No one knows the Son except the Father"* (Mt. 11:27). Our limited minds are not able to fully grasp what it means that He is both *"God over all, blessed forever"* (Rom. 9:5), and at the same time *"the man Christ Jesus"* (1 Tim. 2:5)!

While our Lord lived here on earth, the fullness of the Godhead dwelt bodily in Him. He possessed divine omnipotence and omniscience at all times. But at the same time, as a Man, He learned about human weaknesses and limitations from His own experience. For example, in view of His coming in power and glory, He explained to His disciples, *"But concerning that day or that hour, no one knows, not even the angels in heaven, nor the Son, but only the Father"* (Mark 13:32). When He was ultimately crucified in weakness, He cried in terrible pain, *"my strength is dried up like a potsherd"* (Ps. 22:15).

Many other events show us the same apparent paradox. After a long journey, the Lord Jesus sat exhausted at the well in Sychar. However, Isaiah writes, *"The LORD is the everlasting God, the Creator of the ends of the earth. He does not faint or grow weary"* (Isa. 40:28). He slept in the boat as He crossed the lake with His disciples. The Psalmist, in turn, says that the Keeper of Israel neither slumbers nor sleeps (see Ps. 121:4). Finally, He, Who alone possesses immortality, died on the cross at Calvary (see 1 Tim. 6:16).

The signs and miracles that the Lord performed served as proof that He is truly the Son of God (see John 20:31). His active dependence, on the other hand, made it clear how perfectly He lived here as a true Man.

We must never separate the two sides of the truth that He is God and Man in one Person! We can, however, try to distinguish them in His life with due caution—although even this is often not easy and carries the risk of deceiving ourselves.

He is the almighty Creator and at the same time the One Who, as a dependent Man, was already cast upon God from the womb. We see Him suffering hunger, but also as the One Who fed 5000 men with five loaves of bread and two fish. He was thirsty, although He had the power to turn water into wine. On one occasion He was carried by a boat across the lake, while another time He walked majestically on the raging waters. Every morning He would open His ear in prayer (see Isa. 50:4) to be taught as a disciple or learner. But the same Person ruled with authority over the forces of nature. Although He had no more strength on the cross and His tongue stuck to

His jaws (see Ps. 22:15), He could still cry out with a loud voice, *"It is finished"* (John 19:30)!

The more we reflect on His unique life, the more we will agree with what the Shulammite and the sons of Korah say about Him: He is *"distinguished among ten thousand"* and *"the most handsome of the sons of me"* (see SoS. 5:10; Ps. 45:2)!

We cannot imitate the eternal Son of God in His omnipotence and omniscience. But as a dependent Man He is our Example, and we should become more and more like Him. God created us humans as dependent creatures. Therefore, we can only find lasting fulfillment and satisfaction if we really want to live in dependence on God and in this way answer to the purpose of our existence. This is why the Lord said to His disciples, *"It is enough for the disciple to be like his teacher, and the servant like his master"* (Mt. 10:25).

The word of God calls Him *"the founder and perfecter of our faith"* Who walked the path of dependence before us and has already reached the goal (see Heb. 12:2). Now it's up to us to follow Him on this path. But what does this look like practically in everyday life?

On the one hand the following thoughts are intended to motivate us to learn from our Lord and Master as to what constitutes a dependent life. On the other hand, perhaps they can help us a little in realizing the challenging words of Jesus, Who invites us to *"Abide in me... for apart from me you can do nothing"* (John 15:4–5).

This book is not intended to be read all at once, in one go. Instead, you should rather let the devotions—each one individually—take effect on you in your personal quiet time. The questions that are often asked at the end are intended to stimulate reflection and have the best effect when you take some time to consider them in prayer before the Lord.

Introductory Thoughts

The Joy of a Dependent Life

"I came that they may have life and have it abundantly." (John 10:10)

"Apart from me you can do nothing," (John 15:5) the Lord Jesus once said to His disciples. With this statement He makes it clear that there is only one way we can bear fruit for God: if we remain in Him, the true Vine. But what does this actually mean in practice? How can this be implemented in daily life? How would you answer this question?

Dependence means to be dependent on someone. The word often has a negative connotation for us, because we like to be independent and do not want to be restricted in our freedom. But those who have once experienced how specifically one can experience God's guidance and His work through practiced dependence, come to a completely different conviction: Practiced dependence is the key to a blessed, meaningful and exciting life in fellowship with the living God, Who still does wonderful things today!

A born-again Christian who lives in dependence on God will practice the following three points in his life, which are examined in more detail in this book:

- He shows by his prayer life that he lives in dependence.
- He makes himself dependent on the guidance and power of the Holy Spirit.
- He lives in the expectation that God speaks to him through His living word and thereby gives him guidance.

But what does such a dependent life look like in specific terms? If you want to know this, then you must study the life of the Lord Jesus. The *"founder and perfecter of our faith"* (Heb. 12:2) was always in prayer (see Ps. 109:4), was guided by the Holy Spirit (see Luke 4:1) and lived by every word that comes from the mouth of God (see Mt. 4:4). Because He now lives in you in the power of the Holy Spirit, you are able to walk in His footsteps—and to walk *"in the same way in which he walked"* (1 John 2:6). But you will only be able to do this if you live daily in conscious dependence on Him!

The following devotions should help you to reflect more on the wonderful life of the Lord Jesus. The more thoroughly you do this in prayer, the more you will become like Him in His attitude and behavior—and thus bear fruit that will last for eternity!

"By this my Father is glorified, that you bear much fruit and so prove to be my disciples."
(John 15:8)

Conformed or Transformed?

"Do not be conformed to this world, but be transformed by the renewal of your mind, that by testing you may discern what is the will of God, what is good and acceptable and perfect." (Romans 12:2)

In Romans 12 verse 1 we are told to offer our bodies to God as a living sacrifice. One question we could ask is with what motivation we should do this. The answer is: out of gratitude for the mercies of God, which are described in the first eight chapters. Devotion does not come about through legal pressure, but is the answer to God's love for us, as John aptly writes, *"**We** love because **he** first loved us."* (1 John 4:19).

The Son of God demonstrated His love for the Father by obediently going to Calvary (see John 14:31). His love for each one of us was shown in that He *"gave himself up for us"* (Eph. 5:2). Now we are challenged to be imitators of God and to show our love as the Lord Jesus did—through sacrificial giving (Eph. 5:1–2)!

God longs for a response to His love in your life. The Lord Jesus is looking with holy jealousy for you to give Him the best love (Rev. 2:4). He desires that you surrender yourself to Him without reserve and live in devotion to Him.

This raises the question of what such a life looks like in practical terms and what exactly each of us should do for God. To find this out, we should examine *"what is the will of God, what is good and acceptable and perfect"* for us. This requires dependence.

Paul mentions here in Romans 12:2 two things that help us to live in dependence on God:

1. We should be conformed to the world.
2. We are to be transformed by bringing our thinking into conformity with the thoughts of God.

Before we go into more detail about the dependent life of the Lord Jesus, let's first ask ourselves how we can put the two points just mentioned into practice.

What does Paul actually mean by the term 'world'? What characterizes this 'world' and why is it so dangerous for the children of God? What do the words of John mean, who writes, *"Do not love the world or the things in the world. If anyone loves the world, the love of the Father is not in him."* (1 John 2:15)?

In the following devotions, a brief journey through the history of the Old Testament should help us to understand a little better why this subject is so fundamental for us today.

> *What does it mean for you to offer your life to God as a "living sacrifice"? How does devotion become clearly visible in your life in specific ways? What is it that motivates you to do the will of God?*

Notes:

....

....

....

....

....

....

....

....

....

....

....

....

....

....

....

....

....

Trust or Mistrust? — A Lesson from Paradise

"You are good and do good." (Psalm 119:68)
"Is it even so, that God has said?" (Genesis 3:1)

About 6000 years ago God placed Adam and Eve in a wonderful environment in paradise where they lacked nothing. But although they had the loving care of their Creator before their eyes every day, they doubted His love for them and consciously decided to act against His will.[1] They wanted to be on the same level as God—to be like Him—and to make their decisions independently of Him. Does this sound familiar to you? Isn't it often the case that we fear that God wants to withhold from us what we think is good? Sometimes we are simply afraid that God's will doesn't coincide with our will, and so we hesitate to surrender the reins and let Him take the lead.

Yet today, compared to the first people, we have many more reasons to trust that God has only the best plans for us. Why? Because He proved His love in an incomparable way at Calvary! What does faith conclude from this? *"He [God] who did not spare his own Son but gave him up for us*

---

1   The very moment Eve listened to Satan and turned away from God, she saw that the forbidden tree was good for food, a delight to look at and to be desired to make one wise (see Gen. 3:6). The desires of the flesh, the desires of the eyes and the pride of life characterize this world (see 1 John 2:16) and will inevitably take the lead when God is left out.

all, how will he not also with him graciously give us all things?" (Rom. 8:32). If He has not withheld from us the greatest and dearest Treasure He had, He will give us everything else that is good for us—and He knows this much better than we do! Isn't it rather irrational and inconsistent if we on the one hand trust God for the eternal salvation of our souls, but on the other hand have a certain mistrust that He will also take care of the daily things and that we therefore—as best we can—provide security for ourselves?

The Lord Jesus rested in the love of His Father. The daily awareness of this love was the source of His joy (see John 15:10–11). He trusted Him at all times and therefore could say *"Yes, Father"* even in difficult times (see Mt. 11:25–26). Day and night He turned to Him for guidance and involved Him in every decision of His life (see Ps. 16:7–8).

> *How about you? Do you also rest in the love of God? Do you trust that He has only the best plans for you every day, even if you do not always understand His actions? How does this trust manifest itself in your daily life and in how you make decisions?*

Notes:

....

....

....

....

....

....

....

....

....

....

....

....

....

....

....

....

....

....

....

....

....

....

....

....

....

....

....

....

....

....

Passing Time, or Redeeming the Time? — The Descendants of Cain

"The world is passing away along with its desires, but whoever does the will of God abides forever." (1 John 2:17)

After the fall, the descendants of Cain tried to make their lives as pleasant as possible through possessions, music and inventions of all kinds in order to be happy without God (see Gen. 4). This very attitude is what still characterizes the world today.

How many things people have invented in the last 6000 years that distract them from focusing on what is linked with eternity! Just think of the explosive development of technology and means of communication in the last decades. These things are not evil in themselves and can certainly be used for good, but now they take up much more space in the lives of most of us than we would like. Whereas 20 years ago people were perfectly fine without a cell phone, today many people look at their smartphone on average about a hundred times a day, and they carry it around with them almost everywhere. How much time is lost—time which is actually entrusted to us to rightly spend in the light of eternity!

The Lord Jesus often purposely visited deserted or lonely places in order to be alone (see Luke 4:42) and to seek the will of God in prayer (see Mark 1:35). In the desert and on the mountain He was alone with His Father and found rest—before and after His ministry (see Luke 5:16; Mt. 14:23). Although He served tirelessly and did only good deeds, He was never stressed. He did not live under the tyranny of time!

The Lord told His disciples to close the door behind them to talk to God alone in their chamber. While on the one hand, speaking in the sense of Daniel, we have to open the windows of our hearts to the things of God, at the same time we have to consciously close the door of our heart to everything that keeps us from prayer.

> *A deserted place is a solitary place where there is nothing interesting to distract you. No smartphone, no tablet, no laptop. Where are your 'desert places' where you regularly retreat to calm down and talk to God undisturbed? Have you ever thought about the influence your smartphone has on you? Are you willing to correct yourself regarding the use of social media if you find that frequent use of these things has a negative impact on your spiritual life and distracts you from what has eternal value?*

Notes:

....

....

....

....

....

....

....

....

....

....

....

....

....

....

....

....

....

....

....

....

....

....

....

....

....

....

....

....

The Consumer in these Frenetic Times?

"But godliness with contentment is great gain." (1 Timothy 6:6)

Abel is murdered and Seth is born. He names his son Enosh, which means 'weak' or 'mortal' man. The awareness of their own weakness and dependence drives believers to prayer: "*At that time people began to call upon the name of the LORD*" (Gen. 4:26). The story of the descendants of Cain, on the other hand, is quite different—pride and self-confidence dominate their world. They build cities for themselves and increase their possessions without seeking the will of God (see Gen. 4:17–22).

We're all in danger of making our lives as pleasant as possible in the world where the Son of God became poor and had nowhere to lay His head (see Mt. 8:20).[2] How does this fit together? With just a few clicks, before you know it, you can spend a lot of money on nice things that make your life easier. Do you really take the time to check whether it's God's will or not? How easily doesn't that happen to us—we don't seek God's will and simply adopt the lifestyle of the world! Do we even acknowledge this? The exhortation: *"Do not be conformed to this world"* (Rom.

---

2   The Greek word in this verse for "lay" is the same as "bowed" in John 19:30. The only place here on earth where the Son of God could 'lay' His head was on the cross.

12:2) is a hot topic in our fast-moving consumer-oriented times!

After 4000 years of human history, the Son of God came to earth to dwell or tabernacle among mankind (see John 1:14 JND). As each went to his own house, He went to the Mount of Olives (see John 8:1). There the heavenly Stranger spent many nights, while during the day He devotedly served the people (see Luke 21:37). It was far from His intention to accumulate property in this world. On the contrary, He lived a very modest life, yet He was always satisfied because He had God as His inheritance (see Ps. 16:6).

At the feeding of the 4000, the Lord gave thanks both for the seven loaves of bread and for the few small fish that were brought to Him (see Mark 8:6–7). Another time He took five loaves and two fish, looked up to heaven, dependent and trusting, gave thanks and handed them to His disciples (see Mark 6:41). Although He gave generously in grace, so that there was abundance, He was at the same time careful that nothing was lost and asked His disciples to gather up the remaining leftovers (see John 6:12).

> How does your life show that you're not
> of the descendants of Cain? To what ex-
> tent does your consumerism reflect your
> heavenly outlook on life? Be grateful and
> satisfied for that which God gives you
> daily and abundantly to be enjoyed (see
> 1 Tim. 6:17)!

Notes:

....

....

....

....

....

....

....

....

....

....

....

....

....

....

....

....

....

The World after the Flood—Who Holds the Reins?

"Is the LORD's hand shortened?" (Numbers 11:23)

After God had judged the world through the flood, He made a new start with Noah and his family. But again, the people failed. Instead of obeying their Creator, trusting that He only wanted the best for them, they tried to reach heaven by their own efforts at the Tower of Babel. Their pride even led them so far that they wanted to make a name for themselves and control the population of the earth independently of God (see Gen. 11).

Is this not typical for our time too? People strive to maintain control themselves rather than handing it over to God. What is the situation in your life?

What was Jesus' attitude when He lived here on earth? Among His disciples, He was the Servant Who washed their feet (see Luke 22:27; John 13). He did not seek His own glory here, but sought the glory of the One Who had sent Him (see John 7:18; 8:50). Instead of wanting to control everything Himself, He gave the guidance of His life to the Spirit of God and made Himself dependent on what His Father communicated to Him. Resting in the knowledge that God holds the reins, He said to Pilate, *"You would have no authority over me at all unless it had been given you from above"* (John 19:11).

> *In which areas of life do you find it hard to be humble? Have you consciously handed over the reins of your life so that your Lord can take the lead, or is there something holding you back from this? Are you prepared—trusting fully in Him—to let go even more?*

Notes:

....

....

....

....

....

....

....

....

....

....

....

....

....

....

....

....

The Example of Abraham—Are You an Armchair Christian or an Overcomer?

"In the world you will have tribulation. But take heart; I have overcome the world." (John 16:33)

That the world is a danger for believers, which can have a lasting negative influence on our lives, is made particularly clear by the example of Abraham. As people increasingly devoted themselves to idolatry, God called Abraham out of the world in sovereign grace. He gave him unconditional promises in which the patriarch was to trust (see Gen. 12:1–3).

Then the faith of Abraham was tested by a famine in Canaan—and he failed. Abraham sought refuge in Egypt[3], an image of the world, hoping for a more comfortable life there. But the plan didn't work. His time in Egypt interrupted his fellowship with God—with far-reaching consequences: The possessions he received in Egypt later led to a dispute between the shepherds of Lot and the shepherds of Abraham. How much strife

---

3   Instead of looking upwards to heaven and trusting God would give rain at the right time, the Egyptians looked downward at the Nile irrigating the land. They didn't see the source of the water in the mountains, but only the river itself (see Deut. 11:10–12). The world enjoys the blessings of creation, without seeing the Creator Who is behind it all.

there has been among believers because of possessions and money!

Moreover, Hagar came from Egypt to the promised land. She is a picture of the covenant of the Law (see Gal. 4:21–31), which is considered one of the elements of the world (see Col. 2:8, 20). Legal thinking that wants to achieve the promised blessing of God through its own efforts is completely contrary to the grace of God and cannot bear fruit for God.

In Hebrews 11 we read about the *"treasures of Egypt."* It was on these earthly riches and 'securities' that the Egyptians trusted at that time, and it is exactly these in which people still put their trust today. Financial wealth contains the great danger for believers to act independently of God and to trust more in possessions than in the living God (see 1 Tim. 6:17)!

Are you willing to critically examine how much you rely on financial security and how much you really trust in God?

As Abraham in his day, we're also in great danger of trying to escape the trials through which God allows us to pass by fleeing to Egypt—figuratively speaking—by adapting to the spirit of this world without waiting for God and seeking His will.

In trials of faith the attraction of the world often increases for Christians. How quickly don't we flee to Moab, figuratively speaking, because there's a famine in Bethlehem (see Ruth 1)! Instead of securing food for God's people with the energy of faith, as Gideon did, we rather have the tendency to retreat to our comfortable sofa, from where we judge the weak condition of other believers. It's always easier and more comfortable to retreat or run away when, for example, a local meeting (church) is in a weak spiritual condition, instead of standing firm where God has placed us, depending on the Lord and doing the work of edification!

In the desert, Satan tempted the Lord Jesus with everything this world has to offer. How did the Son of God behave when He was confronted with the desires of the flesh, the desires of the eyes and the pride of life (see Luke 4:1–13)? Although He fasted for 40 days and was hungry, He didn't use His power for His own benefit. He didn't even want to eat anything without receiving an instruction from God. Nor did He take a shortcut on the way to dominion over this world, but remained faithful to God and went through suffering to glory. He also refused to put God to the test lightly, because He did everything in dependence on His Father and trusted Him with all His heart. In the end He resolutely went to Jerusalem knowing that He would not be put to shame (see Luke 9:51; Isa. 50:7).

How do you usually deal with trials that God allows in your life? Are you easily discouraged and try to give up, or do you try to stand firm and edify others where God has placed you? Take Moses as your example—"he endured as seeing him who is invisible" (Heb. 11:27). Be prepared to deny yourself today, to take up your cross and follow the One Who overcame the world!

Notes:

....
....
....
....
....
....
....
....
....
....
....
....
....
....
....

The Renewal of Our Mind—Why Am I the Way I Am?

"We all, with unveiled face, beholding the glory of the Lord, are being transformed into the same image from one degree of glory to another. For this comes from the Lord who is the Spirit." (2 Corinthians 3:18)

Now that we have dealt with some of the dangers of the world, we turn to the positive side of Romans 12:2, *"be transformed by the renewal of your mind."* What does this mean practically for our lives and what can we do to change our thinking?

Our mind, or rather our thinking, is shaped by what we deal with every day—for better or for worse. The things we hear, see or think about influence our inner orientation, even if we may not always be aware of it. This is true of worldly music and films, among other things, as well as many internet sites and forms of social media, which often—without us noticing it—inject us with the world's way of thinking. When we read the Word of God instead and engage with things that have eternal value, our mind-set is renewed and shaped in a positive way.

We can compare this with the daily intake of food: God created humans as dependent creatures who cannot live without food. If someone eats the wrong food or does not eat at all, he becomes weak or sick. This applies to the body as well as to the spiritual life. Just as our outer man needs something to eat every day, so our inner man needs spiritual food every day. How easy it is to forget this in everyday life!

The Lord Jesus called Himself the *Bread of Life* and called on His disciples to feed on Him (see John 6:54–56). But what does this mean for us in practical terms? How do you do this? To eat something means to internalize it, making it part of ourselves. In order to 'internalize' the Lord Jesus, we must engage with Him for example, by studying His life in the four Gospels. How did He behave in the different situations of His life? What did He say and do, and why exactly in this context? Do we find moral qualities of our Lord in the passage we are reading? What can we learn from Him? When we think about Him in this way, we feed our inner man. This in turn has practical implications for our life and thinking: we will then live on account of Him (see John 6:57), i.e. He then becomes the source, motivation and goal for our life and the Person Who shapes and forms us.

These thoughts will probably not be unknown to you. But the question is to what extent you really (today!) put this into practice—because the manna had to be collected daily (see Ex. 16:26–29).

But we don't have to limit ourselves to the Gospels. The epistles also show us many glories of the Son of God that

we should reflect on. For example, we can concern ourselves with the titles that are given to Him there. What
do these titles mean? What is the place like where He is
right now? What is He doing now in glory? When we have
His Person before our eyes in this way, the Holy Spirit
does something wonderful in us: He transforms us more
and more into the image of our Lord (see 2 Cor. 3:18)!

> *What do you do in your spare time? Is the
> topic 'Occupation with the Lord Jesus'
> pious theory, or daily practice for you?
> Ask Him today to help you to become
> more like Him!*

Notes:

....

....

....

....

....

....

....

....

....

....

The Dependent Man

"She gave birth to her firstborn son and wrapped him in swaddling cloths and laid him in a manger." (Luke 2:7)
"He was crucified in weakness." (2 Corinthians 13:4)

God became man and lived among us. What a tremendous truth! The eternal Son of God came as a dependent Child into this world and learned about human limitations and weaknesses from His own experience. Tiredness, exhaustion, hunger, thirst and loneliness are things that He Himself had never experienced before. In the desert He fasted for 40 days and suffered hunger; on the cross He hung in unimaginable suffering and said, *"I thirst."* Exhausted, He sat at the well in Sychar after a long journey on foot. Although the storm raged and high waves battered the ship, He was fast asleep as He crossed the lake with His disciples. Shortly before His death, He looked back once more and said, *"Yet you are he who took me from the womb; you made me trust you at my mother's breasts. On you was I cast from my birth, and from my mother's womb you have been my God."* (Ps. 22:9–10). *"Father, into your hands I commit my spirit!"* (Luke 23:46) were His last words as He hung dying on the cross.

Weakness is not an obstacle for God to use us. On the contrary. God's power is made perfect in weakness (see 2 Cor. 12:9)! The Lord Jesus was crucified in weakness (see 2 Cor. 13:4). There on the cross suffering terrible pain, He said, *"I am a man who has no strength"* (Ps. 88:4), He accomplished the greatest work of His life! It is wonderful that there is now a glorified Man in heaven Who, because of His own experience, can understand us 100% in our weaknesses, and has compassion on us (see Heb. 4:15).

Dependence in the life of Jesus is particularly evident in the three points already mentioned at the beginning, which are also of central importance for us, and which we will deal with more intensively in what follows in the rest of this book:

- Dependence in prayer
- Dependence on the Holy Spirit
- Dependence on the Word of God

> *How should the consciousness of your weakness cause a change in you? Are you aware that you are cast upon God and depend upon Him daily? How does considering that there is Someone in heaven Who truly understands you and has complete compassion for your weaknesses affect your daily life?*

Notes:

....
....
....
....
....
....
....
....
....
....
....
....
....
....
....
....
....
....
....
....
....
....
....
....
....
....

Dependence in Prayer

Dependence and Trust

"Preserve me, O God, for in you I take refuge." (Psalm 16:1)

God is completely independent of every created being. He is the blessed and sole authority, Who does not need anyone in order to be happy, and Who does not have to give account to anyone (see 1 Tim. 6:15). We human beings, on the other hand, are creatures dependent on God, whether we want to admit it or not. How does someone live who is aware that he needs God's help every day? He *prays!* Prayer is practical dependence. But not only that: prayer also expresses trust. We pray because we believe that God hears us and responds to prayer with wisdom. *"Whoever would draw near to God must believe that he exists and that he rewards those who seek him"* (Heb. 11:6).

The Lord Jesus is God and Man in one Person—a wonder that we can't understand, but which we can admire in worship. He commanded the violent storm and it was stilled; the troubled sea and the raging waves obeyed Him, so that suddenly there was a *"great calm"* (Mark 4:39). The Son of God spoke a word and people were instantly healed from their sicknesses. He caused the blind to see, the lame to walk, the deaf to hear and the dumb to speak. Lepers were instantly cleansed and even death was removed when He raised people from the grave (see John 11:43). He said *"I am"* and ranks of His enemies fell to the ground. Even the demons trembled and obeyed His commanding voice. With only five loaves and two fish He fed 5000 men, plus women and children!

The same person looked up humbly to heaven and prayed: *"Preserve me, O God, for in you I take refuge"* (Ps. 16:1). Every day He lived in the awareness that He needed God's protection. Through prayer He rested in the shadow of the Almighty (Ps. 91:1–2).

The fact that Jesus' prayer life was characterized by trust becomes clear in many places: At the tomb of Lazarus He lifted up His eyes and prayed, *"Father, I thank you that you have heard me. **I** knew that you always hear me"* (John 11:41–42). At the time of His arrest, He was absolutely certain that God would place twelve legions of angels at His disposal that very instant, if He would only ask Him (see Mt. 26:53). Even in Gethsemane, where He lay on His face in agonizing prayer, He believed that everything was possible for His Father (Mark 14:36). With unshakable confidence, He prayed in expectation of His resurrection, *"My flesh also dwells secure. For you will not abandon my soul to Sheol, or let your holy one see corruption. You make known to me the path of life"* (Ps. 16:9–11).

We honor God when we trust Him, for in so doing we show Him and others that we consider Him trustworthy. This is one of the reasons why God rejoices when we pray. It honors Him when we trust Him with great things and then ask for them in prayer for His glory!

The Lord Jesus once asked an important question of two blind men who in prayer begged Him for mercy, *"Do you believe that I am able to do this?"* (Mt. 9:28). Sometimes it is good to ask yourself this question when you start praying for something. The prayer of faith has a wonderful promise: *"Therefore I tell you, whatever you ask in prayer, believe that you have received it, and it will be yours."* (Mark 11:24).

> *How do you show God*
> *that you are really dependent on Him?*
> *With what trust do you pray?*
> *Let your life be a visible demonstration*
> *that God is trustworthy!*

Notes:

....

....

....

....

....

....

....

....

....

....

....

Truly Authentic, or More of an Act?

"Behold, you delight in truth in the inward being." (Psalm 51:6)

The evangelist Luke especially shows us the humanity of the Lord Jesus. He is presented there as the praying Man fourteen times—a testimony of His perfect dependence (see Luke 3:21; 5:16; 6:12; 9:16, 18, 28; 10:21; 11:1; 22:17, 32, 41–44; 23:34, 46; 24:30). In no other gospel is it mentioned that He prayed that many times. We'll look at these passages, along with some others, in the next devotions and apply them to our lives.

Having seen, as far as chapter 11, many occasions where the Lord prayed, we will see from then on how He explained the principles of prayer to His disciples. Luke repeatedly makes it clear that in the life of Jesus actions came before teaching, for he writes: *"all that Jesus began to do and teach"* (Acts 1:1).

With our Lord there was no discrepancy between teaching and practice. He lived out what He taught, and He was exactly what He said to people (see John 8:25). His thought went no further than His mouth (see Ps. 17:3). He loved not only with words, but in deed and truth (see 1 John 3:18). His life is also the best example of what it means that we should always pray and not lose heart (see Luke 18:1).

Before preaching the Word of God in the synagogue in Nazareth, He first applied it to Himself in the desert when He was tempted by Satan. It is therefore no wonder that we read that He preached with authority and power—in contrast to the hypocritical scribes (see Mt. 7:28–29).

God wants to see reality and sincerity in our lives! He is looking for people who live out what they profess publicly or preach aloud. As the saying goes, 'Your actions are screaming so loudly, I can't hear what you are saying!' If our lives don't back up what we tell others, then our words or testimony have neither power nor moral authority. For example, if we as Christians profess that we are pilgrims on earth because our true home is heaven, and at the same time make ourselves as comfortable as possible down here, our testimony is not very credible.

> *How much of what you profess or preach is visible in your own life? Is it your heartfelt desire that the discrepancy between doctrinal knowledge and practice in your life is constantly decreasing? How can others see in you that you don't belong to the world, but that your true home is heaven?*

Notes:

....
....
....
....
....
....
....
....
....
....
....
....
....
....
....
....
....
....
....
....
....
....
....
....
....
....

Pray without Ceasing!

"Praying at all times in the Spirit, with all prayer and supplication." (Ephesians 6:18)

The Lord Jesus as Man deliberately took the place of dependence on God. With prayer He began His public service at His baptism—and with prayer He ended it at the cross. He lived praying and He died praying!

What He did for God and for man was done in prayer. He spoke with His Father in seclusion, in the presence of His disciples, in the circle of friends and publicly on the cross. He prayed for Simon Peter, for His disciples, for those who would believe in Him through their word, for His enemies and for Himself. Before and after any completed service we find Him alone in the silence before God. In addition to the times when He withdrew to pray, He lived in a constant attitude of prayer, so that He could say: *"But I give myself unto prayer"* (Ps. 109:4).

God calls us to pray unceasingly (see 1 Thess. 5:17). But how does this actually work? God wants us not only to get on our knees in the morning and then again before going to bed, but also to live in a permanent attitude of prayer throughout the day, in addition to the times when we speak aloud to God. This means that we include God in all of life's situations and keep Him before us in our thoughts. This is how the Lord Jesus lived, Who could say: *"I have set the LORD always before me"* (Ps. 16:8). What an example! How challenging in this context are the words of John: *"Whoever says he abides in him ought to walk in the same way in which he walked."* (1 John 2:6).

> *When you consider your daily prayer life, what conclusions do you come to regarding how dependent on, or independent of, God you're living your life? What can help you in future to go through the day with a more permanent attitude of prayer?*

Notes:

....

....

....

....

....

....

....

....

....

....

....

....

Pray in Every Place!

"I desire then that in every place the men should pray."
(1 Timothy 2:8)

It's the explicit will of God that men pray in every place. The Son of God is our great Example in this regard as well: He prayed at the Jordan, in a barren place, in the desert, on the mountain, at the tomb of Lazarus, in the upper room, in Gethsemane and on Calvary. He had no rigid or legal prayer life which was limited to certain places and certain times of day.

We can see this when we think of His prayer times: He prayed early in the morning before sunrise (see Mark 1:35), in the morning (see Luke 23:34), in the afternoon (see Luke 23:46), in the evening (see Mt. 14:23) and during the night (see Luke 6:12).

God has given men a special responsibility with regard to public prayer. This is especially true of the prayer meetings in the local assembly[4] (church). The Lord Jesus once said with regard to the house of God: *"It is written, 'My house shall be called a house of prayer'"* (Mt. 21:13). God's dwelling place should be marked especially by prayer.

4　The Greek word 'ekklesia'—used in the Word of God mostly to indicate the entirety of all born again Christians locally or globally— is best translated as 'assembly' although the word 'church' is more commonly used in today's language.

Since the sisters are to remain silent in the meetings (see 1 Cor. 14:34), it's the duty of the brothers to pray aloud in the prayer meetings.

Why is it that the prayer meeting in particular is often the least attended meeting of the local assembly—even though the Lord has promised that He will be present when we gather in His name (see Mt. 18:20)? Why are there often such long pauses between prayers? Dear young brother, let the Lord use you to pray aloud in prayer meetings! He rejoices in this. Surely more believers would again be motivated to come to the prayer meetings if prayer were more lively, more specific, shorter and more expectant. You can be an example to others in this too!

By the way, it should also be completely normal for the sisters to pray when we come together as a local assembly—just not out loud. How valuable and effective are the silent prayers of sisters for spiritual guidance and prophetic words in the meetings! It is said of the prophetess Anna that she *"did not depart from the temple, worshiping with fasting and prayer night and day"* (Luke 2:37). This woman's life revolved entirely around the house of God and His interests. She was aware of the failure of the people. But instead of resigning, she served God with devotion and a humble heart.

> *What can you learn from this woman for your life of faith? How can you help to make the 'prayer meetings' of local believers more alive and better attended?*

Notes:

....
....
....
....
....
....
....
....
....
....
....
....
....
....
....
....
....
....
....
....

Prayer Comes before Service

"Jesus... praying... was about thirty years of age." (Luke 3:21, 23)

Even at the age of 12, Jesus was sitting in the temple in Jerusalem—with the conviction that His Father's things were His highest priority. Even then He showed total devotion, which remained unbroken His entire life. There in the temple He listened to the scribes, asked them questions and gave astounding answers when they questioned Him. Since the Gospels tell us nothing else about His childhood or youth, we can probably assume that He did not appear in public during this time. He waited patiently in dependence on God for the time appointed to begin His public ministry.

About 18 years later the Lord Jesus was baptized by John in the Jordan. The calling voice of the Baptist reached its highest point with the announcement: *"Behold, the Lamb of God!"* (John 1:36). Shortly afterwards it was to fall silent—in contrast to the Incarnate Word of God, Whose ministry had just begun!

It's very interesting to see what we're told about the beginning of this new phase in the life of the Son of God. He made no great announcement, did no miracles and did not somehow push Himself to the forefront. Instead He prayed at the beginning of His public ministry when John baptized Him in the Jordan River. The intimate relationship with His heavenly Father was the starting point for His ministry. Everything He did came from this living source of fellowship. In this He is our great Example!

Leonard Ravenhill aptly said, "No Christian's spiritual life is deeper than his prayer life." We can try to display spirituality in front of people, but in *"your room"* (Mt. 6:6), where no one sees us and you're alone with God, all self-portrayal comes to an end. Martin Luther, George Whitefield, John Wesley, David Brainerd, Georg Müller, Hudson Taylor, Dwight Lyman Moody, Charles Studd, David Livingstone, Bakht Singh and many other servants of the Lord were all men of prayer. We know them today because of the things God has done through them. But the reason for this is especially because they often spent time surrendered before God and thus became useful vessels in the Master's hand.

"We will devote ourselves to prayer."
(Acts 6:4)

> *Does every service you undertake also stem from vital fellowship with God? It's mentioned of the Lord Jesus that He first prayed (see Luke 3:21) before He taught the Word of God in the next chapter (see Luke 4:16–19). The apostles also placed prayer before the ministry of the Word and said: "We will devote ourselves to prayer and to the ministry of the word" (Acts 6:4). What are your priorities in serving the Lord? How much do you pray and how much do you serve? What is the danger of reversing the order?*

Notes:

....

....

....

....

....

....

....

....

....

....

....

....

Joy in Heaven

"In your presence there is fullness of joy." (Psalm 16:11)
"Now when all the people were baptized, and when Jesus also had been baptized and was praying, the heavens were opened, and the Holy Spirit descended on him in bodily form, like a dove; and a voice came from heaven, 'You are my beloved Son; with you I am well pleased.'" (Luke 3:21–22)

The dependent attitude that the Lord Jesus showed in prayer brought joy to heaven. His life of prayer was like an altar from which incense was constantly rising (see Ps. 141:2). Proverbs 15:8 explicitly states that the prayer of the upright is acceptable to God. What an incentive for each of us to be more in prayer before God!

At the same time, the Father rejoiced that His Son—the only sinless man on earth—made Himself one with repentant sinners in the Jordan river. This is no different today. God rejoices when we do not go through life self-righteously, but humble ourselves and become one with those who repent.

The Son of God never did anything to get glory from men (see John 8:50). The Father honored Him, and that was enough for Him (see John 8:54). We see this especially in connection with His baptism and the time when He was transfigured on the mountain in front of His disciples. Both times He prayed and both times the Father publicly testified from heaven about His Son and commended Him before men. To His disciples the Lord said: "*If anyone serves me, he must follow me... If anyone serves me, the Father will honor him*" (John 12:26)—a word that's also directed to our hearts!

It's interesting that Luke, who mentions the Lord's prayer at His baptism, reports that the Father addressed Him personally from heaven—and did not speak about Him as Matthew records. In Luke's account He said: "**You** *are my beloved Son, with* **you** *I am well pleased*" (Luke 3:22). The Son spoke to the Father and the Father to the Son. Prayer brings God into life's circumstances—and through this we have fellowship with Him.

In the Old Testament, Moses entered into the most holy place in the tent of meeting (a picture of heaven) where he spoke with God—and God with him (see Num. 7:89). Through the work of the Lord Jesus every believer today already has access to heaven. The way into the sanctuary and into the presence of God is always open to us (see Heb. 10:19)! We don't have to wait until the rapture or the time of our death in order to enter heaven. We already have the opportunity now, every day, to go by the Spirit in prayer to the "*throne of grace*" (Heb. 4:16). How do we appear there? As those who are brought into favor in the Beloved (see Eph. 1:6 JND)—and on whom, therefore, all the good pleasure of God rests!

> *Are you aware that there's joy in heaven if you get down on your knees with a sincere heart, here on earth? Is there anything that prevents you from exercising the great privilege of 'entering' the 'open' heaven? What can help you to enjoy fellowship with God in prayer more consciously, and thereby spark joy in heaven?*

Notes:

....

....

....

....

....

....

....

....

....

....

....

....

....

....

Your First Priority Sets the Tone for the Day

"Rising very early in the morning, while it was still dark, he departed and went out to a desolate place, and there he prayed." (Mark 1:35)

In Mark 1 the schedule of a day in the life of the Lord Jesus is described. Since it was Sabbath, He went to the synagogue in the morning. There He taught with a power that astonished the people. Suddenly an unclean spirit, which had entered into a man, revealed itself. Jesus commanded him to be silent and immediately cast him out.

From the synagogue He went straight to the house of Simon Peter, whose mother-in-law was confined to bed with a high fever. The Lord took time for her. He took her by the hand, lifted her up and delivered her from her illness.

When evening came, after sunset, the whole city was suddenly at the door. Until late at the night He helped everyone who came to Him with their need (see Mark 1:32–34). What a burden it must have been for Him to bear the weaknesses and sicknesses of the many people that evening (see Mt. 8:16–17)! Like no other, He, the only sinless Man, could share the pain and distress of mankind.

Many would have allowed themselves a 'well-earned' night's sleep after such a demanding evening. But the devoted Servant of God still got up before dawn the next morning to be alone with His God: He *"went out to a desolate place, and there he prayed"* (Mark 1:35). Exhaustion or tiredness could not deter Him from beginning the day in fellowship with His Father. There in silence He received guidance and was prepared for the tasks of the day.

> *What is the priority and importance of morning prayer in your life? What things can you do without in the evening in order to get to bed earlier and begin in the quiet of the next morning, in peace with God?*

Notes:

....

....

....

....

....

....

....

....

....

....

....

....

Are Your Ears Open When You Pray?

"Morning by morning he awakens; he awakens my ear to hear as those who are taught. The Lord GOD has opened my ear." (Isaiah 50:4–5)

The faithful Servant of God was in the habit of getting up early in the morning to start the day with prayer. In Psalm 88:13 He says prophetically, *"In the morning my prayer comes before you (comes to meet you)."* Every morning He lived out His dependence on God by having His ear awakened and opened in the quietness of the morning to be taught like a disciple—a learner (see Isa. 50:4–5).

The great and eternal "I AM," the Lord (Yahweh) of the Old Testament, the Creator of heaven and earth, came into this world in the form of a servant and in prayer allowed God to show Him what He should do! Before daybreak, He entered into the presence of God, where He was prepared for the service of the day. There in the silence He received words to revive tired and despondent souls.

The disciples knew where they could find their Master in the early morning hours. When they eventually reached Him, they confronted Him with the words: *"Everyone is looking for you"* (Mark 1:37). With such news, one tends to respond immediately to the desires of those who are asking for us. To say 'no' and thereby disappoint others is often not easy.

But what did the Lord answer His disciples in this situation? He had already been prepared by His time of quietness in the presence of God, and therefore knew what He should do: *"Let us go on to the next towns, that I may preach there also, for that is why I came out"* (Mark 1:38). This was God's will for Him that day—and this will determined His daily routine.

David, the man after God's own heart, had a burning desire for fellowship with his God in the early morning. He longed for God to speak to him at the beginning of the day, for he wrote: *"Let me hear in the morning of your steadfast love, for in you I trust. Make me know the way I should go, for to you I lift up my soul."* (Ps. 143:8). Let this also be your prayer for today!

> *When you reflect on your life, do you find that you are first and foremost before men or before the Lord? The right start to the day makes a big difference. Do you have open ears during your quiet-time in the morning? To what extent do you expect God to speak to you during this time and prepare you for tasks or decisions that come before you in the day ahead?*

Notes:

....

....

....

....

....

....

....

....

....

....

....

....

....

....

....

....

....

....

....

....

....

....

....

....

....

....

....

Expect Answers to Prayer

"O LORD, in the morning you hear my voice; in the morning I prepare a sacrifice for you and watch." (Psalm 5:3)

The Lord Jesus lived in the expectation that God would answer His prayers. With Him, this went so far that He could say publicly in prayer: *"I knew that you always hear me"* (John 11:42).

The Psalmist brought his requests to God in the morning and then watched expectantly for the answer. Habakkuk also had the expectation that God would respond to his prayer, for he said: *"I will take my stand at my watchpost and station myself on the tower, and look out to see what he will say to me"* (Hab. 2:1). In difficult times Micah confessed, *"But as for me, I will look to the LORD; I will wait for the God of my salvation; my God will hear me"* (Mic. 7:7), and Elijah sent his servant seven times to see if the answer to his prayer was coming (see 1 Ki. 18:43).

How often does it happen to us that we pray in the morning and by noon we no longer know what we asked God for in the morning? Yet God rejoices when we expect Him to respond to prayer and therefore consciously look for responses to that prayer. He is the 'Hearer of prayer' (see Ps. 65:2) and we honor Him when we expect Him to respond to prayer!

> *Do you still remember in the evening the requests you brought before God in prayer during the day? How do you expect Him to give you an answer to your prayers, and how does this expectation manifest itself practically in your life? How can you cultivate an attitude of watchfulness for answers to prayer?*

Notes:

....

....

....

....

....

....

....

....

....

....

....

....

....

....

....

....

Pragmatic or Dependent?

"But now even more the report about him went abroad, and great crowds gathered to hear him and to be healed of their infirmities. But he would withdraw to desolate places and pray." (Luke 5:15–16)

If the Lord uses us for a special task and blesses that ministry, there's a danger that we'll attribute at least part of the success to ourselves. As a result we then tend to act recklessly and neglect prayer because we think we are doing quite well. As JB Stoney aptly put it, "We have a tendency to become independent while enjoying the fruits of dependence."

This wasn't the case with the Lord Jesus. After we're shown in Mark 1:35 how He was in dependent prayer before His Father early in the morning, we read shortly afterwards that He healed a leper. There had never been anything like this in Israel before. Many were deeply impressed by this miracle and came to Him in droves to listen to Him and to be healed of their diseases.

This would have been the opportunity to make a big impact on the people. In this situation, many would have simply pragmatically continued with what had just proved to be successful, without asking about the will of God. But what did the Son of God do in this situation? Since His ministry flowed from fellowship with His

Father, He did not seek the glory of men, nor did He let Himself be led by circumstances or opportunities. He knew people's hearts, and He knew that they only wanted to be healed of their physical ailments, but were rejecting the Savior of the soul. Instead of standing in the spotlight before them, He acted in dependence on God, retired to the desert and went back to prayer (see Mark 1:41–45; Luke 5:15–16).

Withdrawn from the people, He entered into the presence of God, where He received guidance for further service. Although He was in prayer at all times (see Ps. 109:4), He always had the desire for special times of communion with His Father. This repeated 'refueling' in the shadow of the Almighty was His highest priority.

> *What do you do after you have been enabled to do a service for God? Do you also—like the disciples—go back into the presence of the Lord, tell Him what you have experienced, and allow Him to guide you afresh (see Luke 9:10)? Do you consider before the Lord whether He wants you to continue as before? In the course of the day, as far as is possible, return to prayer every now and then (Ps. 55:17; 119:164).*

Notes:

Secret Prayer As the Source of Strength

"He who dwells in the shelter of the Most High will abide in the shadow of the Almighty." (Psalm 91:1)

Luke shows us that the prayer of the Lord Jesus in the wilderness (see Luke 5:16) was followed by the power of God in His public ministry: *"the power of the Lord was with him"* (Luke 5:17). Not only here do we see this obvious connection between prayer in secret and power in ministry. In the next chapter too, it says: *"power came out from him"* (Luke 6:19). Again He had given Himself over to prayer shortly before (see Luke 6:12).

Later He prayed on the mountain where Moses and Elijah appeared in glory (see Luke 9:28), and then He was able to cast out a demon—something His disciples (three of whom had fallen asleep on the mountain) were unable to do, because *"this kind cannot be driven out by anything but prayer"* (Mark 9:29).

Among the early Christians, God also responded to prayer with spiritual strength. After they had prayed together with one accord, they then bore witness with power to the resurrection of Jesus (see Acts 4:29–33). Someone once put forward a simple formula that may not be perfectly accurate, but which nevertheless contains much truth: "Much prayer, much power; little prayer, little power; no prayer, no power!" James writes with regard to prayer, *"You do not have, because you do not ask"* (Jas. 4:2).

Christ is the source of strength for every believer. If you want strength, you can get it from Him in prayer. David also experienced this, because he writes, *"On the day I called, you answered me; my strength of soul you increased."* (Ps. 138:3).

We can be sure that God will also answer with strength nowadays, if we get down on our knees more. How quickly today we tend to excuse our own wrongdoing with weakness. Hardly any Christian will deny that he has no strength in himself and instead needs God's strength to do good (see John 15:5). But this doesn't mean that he really lives in dependence on God.

It sounds humble and pious to speak of our weak condition. But there is a great difference between the admission that we have no strength and the living consciousness in the soul that we are without strength. Those who are truly aware of their own weakness are driven to prayer, where the power of God can be found. Then we can also rely with confidence on the promise of the Lord, who said, *"My power is made perfect in weakness"* (2 Cor. 12:9). If we, conscious of our weakness, prayerfully exercise our dependence on Him, then we'll also remain practically in Him, the Vine, and His fruitful power will show itself in us, the branches.

> *What does the awareness of your own weakness produce in you? Are you willing to change things within yourself so that the power of God can become more manifest in your life? Trust that God will answer prayer with power!*

Notes:

....

....

....

....

....

....

....

....

....

....

....

....

....

....

....

....

....

Intensive Prayer before Important Decisions

"In these days he went out to the mountain to pray, and all night he continued in prayer to God." (Luke 6:12)

Each one of us comes to points in life where we have to make important decisions. It was the same in the life of Jesus. One day He was faced with the decision of choosing twelve men from among His disciples. They were to be with Him for more than three years to learn from Him and to be sent out to serve (see Mark 3:13–15).

As a dependent Man, He did not choose as people would normally choose. Who among us would have chosen Judas Iscariot and then even made him treasurer? The Lord said to His disciples, *"Did I not choose you, the twelve? And yet one of you is a devil"* (John 6:70). He also knew that another disciple would deny Him three times, and that all of them would eventually leave Him and fall away because of Him—and this at the most crucial hour of His life (see Mt. 26:31; John 16:32)!

What did our Lord and Master do before He made this momentous decision? He spent the whole night in prayer (see Luke 6:12–13). For several hours He sought the face of God and talked with Him. Although He was very busy during the day, He still found time to pray again and again. What a challenging example of true dependence!

His perseverance in prayer was the result of His heart's deep desire and not simply a matter of strong self-discipline. He didn't look at the clock or force Himself to do something that was actually a burden for Him. How quickly we feel that we have to struggle to pray longer because we make time our goal and are not exclusively focused on prayer requests or communion with God!

If our Lord spent so much time in prayer before making important decisions, how much more should we do so! Are there times when you spend 30 or 60 minutes alone in prayer? What keeps you from consciously taking a longer time for prayer? Of course, it is unlikely that overnight you will start praying for several hours a day, if on average your daily prayer time is currently 15 minutes. But prayer is like a muscle that becomes more powerful through daily training!

But it could also be that something is so burning in your soul that you don't even notice how time passes while you are spreading it out before the Lord in prayer. And when we've had encouraging experiences in prayer, it can suddenly motivate us to spend more time on our knees, even though we are not really used to it.

> *To what extent are you striving to become more like your Lord and Master also in regard to His prayer life? How much time do you take for prayer when you're faced with important decisions? During prayer, try not to think about time, but focus on your concerns and fellowship with the Lord!*

Notes:

....

....

....

....

....

....

....

....

....

....

....

....

....

....

....

Watch and Pray!

"All night he continued in prayer to God." (Luke 6:12)
"All these with one accord were devoting themselves to prayer."
(Acts 1:14)

All night long the Son of God remained in prayer. What would He have discussed with His Father during these hours? When He was in great distress in Gethsemane about three years later, it seems that He sought the face of His Father three times that night, each time for one hour (see Mark 14:35–41). He not only preached on the subject of prayer, but also lived it out—and He did so until the end of His life.

Christianity began with 120 people who unanimously persevered in prayer, claiming that God would fulfill His promises (Acts 1:14; Luke 11:13; Luke 24:49). How powerfully God responded to this persistent prayer! He loves it when we remind Him of His promises and ask Him to make them a reality in our lives (see Isa. 62:6–7).

Paul writes to the Colossians: *"Continue steadfastly in prayer, being watchful in it with thanksgiving"* (Col. 4:2). We can do this both alone and collectively. Three disciples were together when the Lord told them to watch and pray (see Mt. 26:41). It's sometimes easier to have longer prayer times together with others. This can be done privately or as a local gathering. Especially in those times, when there is a particular need, it is a blessing to come together before the throne of grace, trusting that the 'Hearer of prayer' (Ps. 65:2) will not leave prayers unanswered.

The night after King Herod had Peter thrown into prison, there was light in one of the houses of Jerusalem. Many were gathered there to intercede for their brother in prayer; *"but earnest prayer for him was made to God by the church"* (Acts 12:5). The Lord honored this in a very evident way!

Throughout the history of the Church, believers have repeatedly prayed together through the night. The Lord has often given revival and conversions in response. For example, the Indian evangelist Bakht Singh (1903–2000) spent 19 nights with his co-workers in prayer, with a two-day break, before a three-month crusade in the Chennai area (South-East India). The result was overwhelming blessing that was apparent through many conversions and the formation of assemblies.[5]

The local fellowship groups of the *Herrnhuter Brüdergemeinde* also spent nights in prayer, praying earnestly for the Lord of the harvest to send out workers into His harvest. By the time Zinzendorf, who was a leader of this movement, passed away, about 226 missionaries had gone out to preach the gospel of grace to the whole world!

---

5   TE Koshy, *Brother Bakht Sing of India*, OM Books, Andhra Pradesh, p. 181

> *Do you think that the Lord could still do great things today if we were once again willing to devote ourselves more to prayer and spend several hours together on our knees? Perhaps other believers around you are willing to prove God in this way (see Mal. 3:10), and there is just one person needed who, dependent on the Lord, takes the initiative to start a prayer group. Are you willing to let God use you, and to encourage others to do such "good works" (see Heb. 10:24)?*

Notes:

....
....
....
....
....
....
....
....
....
....
....
....
....

Persevering in Prayer

"All night he continued in prayer to God." (Luke 6:12)
"Arise, cry out in the night, at the beginning of the night watches! Pour out your heart like water before the presence of the Lord!" (Lamentations 2:19)

It often takes some time to pour out our soul in peace before the Lord and tell Him everything that is bothering us. The Lord Jesus sometimes spent a great many hours in this way. The Word of God also gives us a whole number of examples of men and women who prayed with perseverance.

It is said of Hannah that she prayed at length before the LORD (see 1 Sam. 1:12)—and how wonderfully He answered! Of her son Samuel we read that he once cried out to the LORD all night long (see 1 Sam. 15:11). God wrestled all night in Peniel with Jacob, and Jacob with Him. The patriarch did not let Him go until he received the blessing at dawn and thus became 'Israel', a *"warrior of God"* (see Gen. 32:24–29). The prophetess Anna was also a woman of prayer, who served night and day with fasting and prayer (see Luke 2:37). Elijah, the man of God, remained in prayer until his servant, who went to look for an answer seven times, finally told him that he saw a cloud on the horizon (see 1 Ki. 18:42–44). In this context, James writes, *"The effective, fervent prayer of a righteous man avails much"* (James 5:16 NKJV)!

It is good, after having cast all burdens on the Lord in prayer, to remain with Him a little longer to see what He places on our hearts, or rather, how He wishes to speak to us in the quiet. When we remain before God like this, it's also a time when the Holy Spirit can explore our hearts and re-adjust our thoughts. Moses often spent time in the tent of meeting, in the presence of God. There he talked with God and God talked with him (see Num. 7:89). Abraham still remained before the Lord after the two angels had turned away to go to Sodom (see Gen. 18:22). In the presence of God, this hero of faith suddenly began to wrestle for souls with much boldness in prayer.

> *Have you ever wrestled with God in prayer for souls? When was the last time you quietly poured out your soul before the Lord Jesus? Take another moment, after having done this, to wait and see if the Lord still has something to say to you!*

Notes:

....

....

....

....

....

....

Doing the Right Thing at the Right Time

"On their return the apostles told him all that they had done. And he took them and withdrew apart to a town called Bethsaida. When the crowds learned it, they followed him, and he welcomed them and spoke to them of the kingdom of God and cured those who had need of healing." (Luke 9:10–11)

It was supposed to have been a day of rest and relaxation. But everything turned out quite differently to what they expected. For the disciples of Jesus it became a day in which they worked as much as if not more than ever before.

What had happened? The Lord Jesus had retired with His disciples to Bethsaida so that the twelve could recover from their ministry in the villages there. But when the crowds heard where they were staying, they immediately ran after them. How did the Son of God react to this? He never complained, nor did He become displeased in any way. Instead, He took the people in and met each one (individually) according to their needs. How many times He accepted sudden interruptions due to an immediate need with much patience and gentleness—and without negative feelings in His heart!

The Lord did not make a legal matter out of quiet times. We never hear Him say, "This is my time of prayer. Come back later." He was always available for people. He used the given time of each day like no one else, but without ever being stressed. The deep fellowship He enjoyed with His Father at all times was so real, that the interruption of a time of quiet never caused Him a crisis.

How balanced our Lord was here on earth! In Him, God found everything He wanted in the life of a man, and at the same time, through Him, God could fully reveal what He wanted to be for mankind. The people who come to God frequently and spend much time in His presence are often those who are most accessible to their fellow men. No one has ever been closer to people than the Man from heaven. Duty says, "There is time for God and time for man." Love says, "There is time—and there always will be—for the good works He has prepared beforehand."

Of course there are also daily duties, whether at work or at home, which we have to perform and which require us to be on call at all times. But the question is, what do we do in our own time?

While, on the one hand, service among people and our daily duties shouldn't interfere with our time in secret with God; on the other hand, the insistence on rest and seclusion should not isolate us from other people. Piety that does not show itself in deeds is dangerous! This doesn't mean that we must respond to every request that is made to us. The Lord Jesus didn't do that either, because He also needed times of rest and retreat. It's rather a matter of doing what God wants us to do in every-thing—regardless of whether we withdraw to refuel or whether we serve actively. It requires dependence to be shown in each new circumstance what the right course of action is in that moment.

> *What will your reaction be when you are unexpectedly asked for help today, although you had actually planned to do something else? Do you tend to neglect service to people, or rather your quiet time before the Lord? One time the Lord said to Elijah, "Hide yourself" and another time, "Show yourself" (1 Ki. 17:3; 18:1). What is He telling you at the moment?*

Notes:

....

....

....

....

....

....

....

....

....

....

Blessing through Prayer

"Taking the five loaves and the two fish, he looked up to heaven and said a blessing over them. Then he broke the loaves and gave them to the disciples to set before the crowd. And they all ate and were satisfied. And what was left over was picked up, twelve baskets of broken pieces." (Luke 9:16–17)

Toward the end of the day the disciples urged their Master to finally dismiss the crowd. But this was not in line with His thoughts. The *"Bread of life"* (John 6:35, 48) didn't want to send the hungry people away with rumbling stomachs. Instead, He tested the faith of the twelve by saying, *"You give them something to eat"* (Luke 9:13). Living faith is demonstrated, among other things, by trusting that God multiplies what little we have in His mighty hand and uses it to bless others. David also prayed with this trust and said: " *In your hand are power and might, and in your hand it is to make great and to give strength to all"* (1 Chron. 29:12).

But instead of trusting their Lord and Master with all their heart, and accepting this commission, the disciples relied on their understanding. This often leaves God out of the picture, and we depend only on what is visible (see Prov. 3:5). We can also apply this to our lives. How do you react when the Lord gives you a commission that far exceeds your capacities?

A little boy, who had five loaves of bread and two fish, was prepared to give them to the Lord. How often has the sacrifice of an individual become a blessing for many! Out of love for her Lord, Mary broke the very precious alabaster flask containing the precious nard and used it to anoint the Son of God. Through her devotion the whole house was filled with the perfume of the anointing oil. Barnabas also used his personal possessions to bless others; selflessly the *"Son of encouragement"* (Acts 4:36) sold a field so that the proceeds could be used for the needs of the believers.

The Lord Jesus took into His hands the little that the disciples brought to Him. Then He turned His eyes to heaven with trust—two glances met (see Ps. 34:15)—and He thanked the Father, from Whom every good gift comes. Later, when He taught His disciples to pray, He said, *"When you pray, say... Give us each day our daily bread"* (Luke 11:2–3). He did not take food for granted, but knew that man depends on the goodness of God every day. In the Gospel of Mark, when feeding the 4000 men, we see that He even prays a second time for the fish (see Mark 8:6–7). The deliberate prayer for seemingly small things is often connected with great blessings and increases our joy and gratitude!

Under the blessing of Jesus and the thanks He gave to God, the five loaves and the two fish were multiplied in a wonderful way, so that no one had to go home hungry.

But not only that—at the end of the day, there were even 12 baskets of bread left over—one for each person who allowed the Lord to use them. The following principle of God is still fully valid in our day: *"One gives freely, yet grows all the richer... Whoever brings blessing will be enriched, and one who waters will himself be watered"* (Prov. 11:24–25).

> *To what extent are you aware that you can only accomplish the tasks God gives you when God gives you the means or the strength to do them (see 2 Cor. 9:8; 1 Pet. 4:11)? In what areas have you already made personal sacrifices to be able to be a blessing to others? Pray consciously also for the small things of everyday life!*

Notes:

....

....

....

....

....

....

....

....

....

Perfectly Timed!

"Immediately he made the disciples get into the boat and go before him to the other side, while he dismissed the crowds. And after he had dismissed the crowds, he went up on the mountain by himself to pray. When evening came, he was there alone." (Matthew 14:22–23)

The Son of God calmly took time to dismiss the crowds in peace. When, because of their full stomachs (see John 6:15), they suddenly wanted to make Him King in spontaneous enthusiasm, He withdrew alone to the mountain to pray there. When temptation comes, prayer is always a reliable weapon to resist the devil!

How much time will He have spent in prayer that evening? Certainly He prayed on the mountain for His disciples who were fighting the waves on the stormy lake during that time. That same Jesus (see Acts 1:11; Eph. 4:10) Who went up on the mountain to pray for His disciples on that occasion, is now—at this moment—acting as High Priest at the right hand of God for you (see Heb. 7:25). Do you reflect on this from time to time?

The next thing we're told about Him is that He met the disciples on the lake in the fourth watch of the night, that is, between 3 and 6 o'clock in the morning. Although He knew that they had already been in great trouble for several hours, He was waiting in prayer for the right time to come to their aid—that is true dependence! He could have commanded the wind and the waves with *one* word from the mountain, but He didn't. Instead, He wanted His disciples to experience that He would meet them at the right time in their need, to help them in mercy and grace (see Heb. 4:16).

One of the reasons God allows trials and opposition in our lives is so that we can (re)focus our gaze on Him alone. In times of need He wants us to get to know Him better and grow spiritually as a result. Like the disciples, we too can learn by faith that He is truly the Son of God, who is above every problem, opposition and fear that we face (see Mt. 14:33).

> *With every trial He allows, God is working in your life for good! Trust that, at the right time—which He alone knows—He will also intervene in your current challenges (see 1 Pet. 5:6)! Have you ever come to the point where you were so overwhelmed by the solutions the Lord Jesus provides, that you could say with the conviction of faith, "Truly, you are God's Son"?*

Notes:

Overcoming through Prayer

"Peter answered him, 'Lord, if it is you, command me to come to you on the water.' He said, 'Come.' So Peter got out of the boat and walked on the water and came to Jesus." (Matthew 14:28–29)

Prayer preserves us from resignation and at the same time helps us to overcome circumstances that are likely to depress us (see Phil. 1:19). This is what Peter also experienced when, on the raging lake, he felt the desire to be very close to his Lord (Mt. 14:28). What a courageous prayer this man prayed in these circumstances! He was prepared to give up human security in order to come closer to his Lord—to be with Him. But for this Peter needed a clear instruction from Him.

Through prayer we can obtain courage to let go and take steps of faith. How happy the Lord must have been to see someone who trusted Him wholeheartedly and had the desire to come to Him on the water! Only when Peter actually set foot on the water did he experience how the Lord carried him—an experience he would never have had if he had stayed in the boat, and which he certainly would not forget his whole life.

Sometimes we're afraid of putting ourselves in a situation where we're completely dependent on God, because we fear that at some point our faith will fail and, for example, we will lose face in front of others. How quickly it happens that someone is called reckless or irresponsible just because, trusting in God, they do something unusual, something that others may simply lack the courage to do!

When he was on the water, Peter actually began to doubt at one point. Suddenly all he saw was the strong wind and the waves in front of him. He lost eye contact with his Master and slowly began to sink—although he still had enough time to ask the Lord for help. At the short prayer, *"Lord, save me,"* the hand of the Son of God was immediately there to pull him out of the water. As Isaiah writes in another context, *"Behold, the LORD's hand is not shortened, that it cannot save,"* (Isa. 59:1).

The Lord doesn't let those who trust in Him drown. He didn't reproach Peter because of his bravery in climbing out of the ship. No, instead He rebuked him for his little faith. Do you also wish you had the confidence to pray a prayer like Peter's, or would you have criticized him from the boat when he suddenly began to sink? Let's not criticize others for steps of faith for which we may simply lack courage. Paul writes, *"Who are you to pass judgment on the servant of another? It is before his own master that he stands or falls. And he will be upheld, for the Lord is able to make him stand"* (Rom. 14:4).

> *Do you long to know your Lord better through practical experiences of faith? Are you ready, if He wills it, to leave your familiar surroundings and set out on 'unknown waters' where you are entirely thrown upon Him? What is stopping you from asking Him whether that is what He wants you to do? We often have so few real experiences of faith because we so seldom ask the Lord to give us a specific commission of this kind!*

Notes:

....
....
....
....
....
....
....
....
....
....
....
....
....
....

Prayer and Discipleship

"It happened that as he was praying alone, the disciples were with him... He said to them... 'The Son of Man must suffer many things and be rejected by the elders.'" (Luke 9:18, 22)

After the Lord Jesus had provided food for 5000 men, Luke shows Him again as a dependent man in prayer. In chapter 9 verse 18 a new section in this Gospel begins. Although Christ, as the LORD (Yahweh) of the Old Testament, provided His people with bread (see Ps. 132:15), He was nevertheless rejected as Messiah by the mass of the people.

From that moment on, in prayer, He took the place of the One Who was rejected. He then spoke openly for the first time to His disciples about the sufferings that awaited Him in Jerusalem. From then on the disciples were no longer to proclaim Him as the Christ (Messiah). His way led through suffering to glory—and this is also the way of every disciple who wants to follow Him today (see Luke 9:23)!

We're only able to deny ourselves, to take up our cross daily, and to follow the Son of God if we realize our dependence on Him every day in prayer. The grace and strength we need to follow Him is found in practical fellowship with God. If we don't realize and live out this fellowship in practice, through prayer and the study of

God's Word, discipleship quickly becomes an empty routine or a legal constraint. This is why our prayer life, especially with regard to daily discipleship, is so fundamentally important!

Consistent discipleship is connected with opposition from the world. Unfortunately, however, experience shows that the headwind often comes from 'our own ranks.' Paul writes, *"Indeed, all who desire to live a godly life in Christ Jesus will be persecuted"* (2 Tim. 3:12). How important it is that we, as born-again Christians, stand together as one—like one man! As brothers and sisters in Christ, and as disciples of the Lord Jesus, we can pray together and thereby strengthen each other's hands for good. Instead of biting and devouring one another (see Gal. 5:15) and going through life as lone fighters, God wants us to have love for one another and to be of one heart and one mind.

When the first Christians were threatened from outside, this drove them to pray together, raising their voices to God *with one accord* (see Acts 4:24). Prayer welds together—and moves the arm of the Almighty!

> **"Is anyone among you suffering? Let him pray."**
> **(James 5:13)**

> *Is following after the Lord Jesus more of a*
> *compulsion or a privilege for you (see Acts*
> *5:41; Phil. 1:29)? How do you show your*
> *love for those who are born of God and*
> *belong to His family? Try, as far as possible,*
> *to pray more together with other disciples*
> *of the Lord!*

Notes:

....

....

....

....

....

....

....

....

....

....

....

....

....

....

....

....

Prayer Opens Your Eyes

"It happened that as he was praying alone, the disciples were with him... Then he said to them, 'But who do you say that I am?' And Peter answered, 'The Christ of God.'" (Luke 9:18, 20)

After the Lord Jesus had prayed, He immediately asked His disciples what they thought about Him. He wanted to hear from them who He was for them. Peter received a divine revelation and recognized in Him the *"Christ, the Son of the living God"* (see Mt. 16:16). It may well be that among other things, that is exactly what the Lord prayed for.

Today, we too are dependent on God to open our eyes so that we may understand the truth and grow in the knowledge of the Son of God (see 2 Pet. 3:18). This is why Paul also prays that the Ephesians would be enlightened in the eyes of their hearts (see Eph. 1:18).

Have you ever had the experience that you suddenly see a verse or passage with different eyes, one that you have read perhaps fifty times before, and something in that scripture suddenly becomes wonderfully clear or significant for you? After he had already been serving as a missionary in China for several years, Hudson Taylor's eyes were opened regarding John 15:1–5 and his life was never the same again. Suddenly this man of God, in faith, realized that Christ lived in him and that it was not a matter of his own efforts, but of letting the Son of God work through him.

God answered Moses' request, when he prayed, *"Please show me your glory"* (Ex. 33:18). He still rejoices today when we have the desire to know Him better and, like Paul in prayer, ask, *"Who are you, Lord?"* (Acts 9:5).

We live today in the time of Laodicea, which is characterized by complacency and indifference with regard to spiritual matters. For this very reason, we should ask the Lord to open our eyes to our personal and collective spiritual condition. This is the first step toward a revival (see Rev. 3:18).

When the boy who was with Elisha saw the great power of the enemy around him, fear overtook him. Elisha, however, was completely calm in the situation. His eyes were open to the spiritual world that surrounded them. Therefore He said, *"Do not be afraid, for those who are with us are more than those who are with them."* Then the man of God prayed, *"O LORD, please open his eyes that he may see."* What was God's answer to this prayer? *"So the LORD opened the eyes of the young man, and he saw, and behold, the mountain was full of horses and chariots of fire all around Elisha"* (2 Ki. 6:15–17).

Do you sometimes pray as the Psalmist, "Open my eyes, that I may behold wondrous things out of your law" (Ps. 119:18)? Pray that God will show you something of His glory today! Remind yourself (again) that besides the visible world, there is also an invisible one, in which spiritual battles take place (even today) which have a mighty influence on your life (see Eph. 6:12)!

Notes:

....

....

....

....

....

....

....

....

....

....

....

....

....

....

Conquering through Hope

"'I tell you truly, there are some standing here who will not taste death until they see the kingdom of God.' Now about eight days after these sayings he took with him Peter and John and James and went up on the mountain to pray. And as he was praying, the appearance of his face was altered, and his clothing became dazzling white." (Luke 9:27–29)

We read quite often that the Lord went up a mountain to pray there (see Luke 6:12; 22:39–41; Mt. 14:23). The mountain speaks on the one hand of separation from people and on the other hand of nearness to God. Whoever climbs a mountain leaves the valley behind for a while to be alone and to have a wider perspective. From the mountain, figuratively speaking, you can see some things a little more through the eyes of God (see Deut. 34:1).

The path Jesus took led through suffering to glory. On this path He, as a dependent Man, also needed encouragement. Psalm 110 verse 7 prophetically says of Him, *"He will drink from the brook by the way; therefore he will lift up his head."* The scene on the Mount of Transfiguration was certainly such a drinking from the stream of God, which is, for us also, always full of water (see Ps. 65:9). He discussed there with Moses and Elijah His departure, which He was about to accomplish at Jerusalem. What an encouragement to know that at that moment the eyes of heaven were on Him. Shortly afterwards it is said,

"When the days drew near for him to be taken up, he set his face to go to Jerusalem." (Luke 9:51).

The *"founder and perfecter of our faith"* had His future glory constantly before the eyes of His heart. This hope helped Him to endure rejection, persecution and suffering here on earth, because we read that, *"who for the joy that was set before him endured the cross, despising the shame"* (Heb. 12:2).

It should be the same with His disciples. After theLord had presented them with the cost of discipleship, God gave them, immediately afterwards on the mountain, a wonderful prophetic vision of future events. Years later, Peter thought back on this and took courage for the last steps that lay ahead of him on the way to his martyrdom (see 2 Pet. 1:14–19). The same Apostle writes, *"We have the prophetic word more fully confirmed, to which you will do well to pay attention as to a lamp shining in a dark place, until the day dawns and the morning star rises in your hearts"* (2 Pet. 1:19).

Now we suffer in this accursed world while we follow a rejected Christ. But soon—perhaps even today—He will come again to take us to His Father's house, the eternal dwelling place of God. We also wait for the day when He, Who was rejected and crucified here, will rule over this creation in power and glory—and that with us at His side! God wants us to be occupied with the future events that He tells us about in His Word. He wants us to know the things that are waiting for us at the end of the road. The anticipation of this spurs us on to be victorious conquerors every day!

> *Often the anticipation of the next holiday helps us to pick ourselves up once more, and to tackle the remaining jobs as well as we can. Is that also true in terms of eternity? To what extent does the hope that you will soon be forever with Christ and that God will wipe every tear from your eyes, have an effect on your life today? Do you have moments when you leave the 'valley' behind you for a few minutes to go to the 'mountain' to talk to God about His interests and goals?*

Notes:

....

....

....

....

....

....

....

....

....

Transformation through Prayer

"As he was praying, the appearance of his face was altered, and his clothing became dazzling white." (Luke 9:29)

While the Lord was praying, He was glorified before the eyes of His disciples. The intention was prayer, but the result was glory (see Luke 9:28). When we apply this scene on the mountain to ourselves, we see two things that happen through prayer:

1. Prayer changes, first of all, the person who prays.
2. Through prayer God shows us something of His glory.

When we pray, we enter heaven in spirit. We enter into the presence of God where the throne of grace is. The presence of God forms us and leaves a lasting impression. How many believers have experienced that after a time of prayer they were changed—and suddenly had peace and joy in their hearts again.

Hannah prayed and wept before the LORD for a long time. After she had poured out her heart to Him, her face was no longer sad (see 1 Sam. 1:10, 18). Moses spent 40 days and nights in the presence of God, and as a result His face shone (Ex. 34:29). God wants to do a work in us before He does a work through us!

Often God shows us something of His glory or His glorious action in response to prayer. *"Please show me your glory."* (Ex. 33:18), Moses prayed in the wilderness, and this was wonderfully answered. Now—as he stands on the mountain in the promised land—he no longer sees the glory of God only from behind, but in the face of a dependent Person—the Lord of glory. This praying Man will one day rule over this earth as *"King of kings and Lord of lords."* Moses didn't pray in vain, and so it will be for us too, if we ask God to reveal His glory in our lives. The Man on the mountain is still the Man who can move mountains today!

The disciples fell asleep while the Lord Jesus prayed and was transformed. When Peter finally woke up, he immediately wanted to start building three tents. In Gethsemane, the Lord told the disciples to wake up and pray. But there too they were overcome by sleep. Shortly afterwards Peter impulsively struck out with his sword to defend his Master. Both times it was—although well-intentioned—misguided activism due to a lack of prayer.

Similar to what happened at His baptism at the Jordan, on the mountain where He was transfigured, prayer was followed by the public testimony of the Father about the Son. The Son of God honored His Father through dependence and trust in prayer, and received glory and honor from Him (see 2 Pet. 1:17). The Lord promised His disciples, *"If anyone serves me, he must follow me; and where **I** am, there will **my** servant be also. If anyone serves me, the Father will honor him"* (John 12:26).

> *What effect does the following promise of God have on your prayer life: "Draw near to God, and he will draw near to you" (Jas. 4:8)? The man who in his time was the meekest man on earth (see Num. 12:3) spent much time in the presence of God. How often do you linger there to be changed by Him? Ask God to make His glory visible in your life too!*

Notes:

....
....
....
....
....
....
....
....
....
....
....
....

Prayer and Fasting

"He said to them, 'This kind cannot be driven out by anything but prayer.'" (Mark 9:29)

When the Son of God descended from the Mount of Transfiguration, He was immediately confronted with the failure of His disciples. How had they failed? Outwardly, the failure consisted in their inability to cast out a particular demon. But this failure had a deeper reason—the Lord explained to them that their lack of faith had been the problem. He had expected them to show more faith in this situation. But how could they have done so? Through prayer and fasting!

Doesn't this example show us that the confidence of faith, which is also shown through prayer and fasting, is blessed by God with special power? Can it therefore be that there are certain problems that God only solves when we pray and fast with faith on our side?

Fasting means first and foremost not eating. In addition, the Word of God also shows us other types of fasting (see Isa. 58:6–7); but the primary way is to abstain from food for a while. While in prayer we express our dependence on God, fasting is an act of self-denial—we give up something we actually need.

In many places in His word, God shows us that God-fearing men and women fasted. Usually it was done in conjunction with prayer; sometimes to humble oneself before God (see Dan 9:3; Ezra 8:21), and sometimes to receive guidance from Him (see Acts 13:1–4). In this way, believers in both the Old and New Testaments allowed their bodies to share in the spiritual trials of the soul.

The Lord Jesus—our great Example—also fasted here on earth. In the same Psalm in which He prophetically says: *"But I give myself to prayer,"* He also says: *"My knees are weak through fasting"* (Ps. 109:4, 24). Forty days and nights—for almost six weeks!—He fasted in the desert, not eating any food. His words, *"This kind cannot be driven out by anything but prayer,"* indicate that He also fasted later, during His public ministry.

Although the Son of God didn't call His disciples to fast in Matthew 6 (just as He didn't call them to pray or give alms here), it seems that He assumed that they would practice it. It's true that throughout the New Testament we find no specific invitation to fast. Nevertheless, Paul, who himself often fasted (see 2 Cor. 11:27), writes that we prove ourselves to be servants of God by fasting (see 2 Cor. 6:5 NKJV).

With regard to the question as to whether fasting is appropriate for Christians today, Christian Briem once aptly said the following, "Do the needs of the Lord's work still occupy and press us so much that we allow our body to participate in the exercises (trials) of the soul? The example of the Apostle and his co-workers (see Acts 13:1–4) shows us vividly what devoted service to the Lord means, and that the body is also touched by it—in waking and fasting."[6]

> *Have you ever asked yourself why God, in His Word, presents to you so many encouraging examples of people who have fasted? There are many who lament the decline of Christianity today; but how many are there who really humble themselves, in deed and in truth—with fasting and pleading? If God has so often responded in grace, why should He not do so today?*

Notes:

....

....

....

....

....

....

....

....

6   *Ermunterung und Ermahnung*, 1991, CSV-Verlag, Hückeswagen, p. 341

An Inner Attitude of Prayer

"'Nevertheless, do not rejoice in this, that the spirits are subject to you, but rejoice that your names are written in heaven.' In that same hour he rejoiced in the Holy Spirit and said, 'I thank you, Father, Lord of heaven and earth, that you have hidden these things from the wise and understanding and revealed them to little children; yes, Father, for such was your gracious will.'" (Luke 10:20–21)

What God has done and is doing for us is always greater and more important than what we are allowed to do for Him. He first wants to do a work in us, and then to work through us. His grace always comes first! We should therefore rejoice much more in what He does for us than in our service to Him. For this reason, the Lord Jesus also told His disciples that they should rejoice much more over the fact that their names were written in heaven, than over the fact that demonic spirits were subject to them.

The Son of God came in grace to His people as the promised Messiah. He was commissioned by His Father to go from village to village to preach the gospel, cast out demons and heal the sick. But although He faithfully fulfilled this commission, the people rejected Him and His message. How did He react to this?

At this point we are told for the first time what the Lord Jesus said to His Father in prayer, *"I thank you, Father."* Is that not remarkable? In these adverse circumstances, He praised His Father and thereby glorified Him (see Ps. 50:23). Moreover, in prayer He had the greatness of God before His eyes, joyfully acknowledged His authority and submitted Himself to His will. This was the mindset and attitude of heart with which He prayed. A challenging example for us!

The Son of God rejoiced with all His heart over the weak and despised of society whom the Father had chosen, those whom He now drew to Him in grace (see 1 Cor. 1:26–29). Children were also especially dear to His heart. That's why He said to His disciples, *"Let the little children come to me and do not hinder them, for to such belongs the kingdom of heaven"* (Mt. 19:14). He was approachable to everyone who came to Him in faith. However, He often stayed with the lowly who were outcasts from society but recognized their sinfulness. His opponents took this as an opportunity to accuse Him of being a friend of tax collectors and sinners (see Mt. 11:19).

While the Pharisees and scribes boasted of the Law, the Lord boasted of the grace of God that opened children's eyes as to Who He was. He praised the wisdom of the Father, Who had decided in His purposes that a rejected Christ should be the door into the presence of God for these people. Peter and John, for example, were unlearned and uneducated people, but their names are written in heaven (see Acts 4:13). How many 'unknown people' are there in the world, but who are *"well known"* in heaven (see 2 Cor. 6:9)!

> *What is your mind more occupied with—what the grace of God has done and is doing for you, or what you are allowed to do for God? In view of the circumstances that God allows in your life, can you also say "Yes, Father" or, "The Rock, his work is perfect, for all his ways are justice" (Deut. 32:4)? How does your life show that you stand up for the lowly and care for those who have nothing with which to repay you (see Rom. 12:16; Luke 14:13–14)?*

Notes:

....

....

....

....

....

....

....

....

....

Lord, Teach Us to Pray!

"Jesus was praying in a certain place, and when he finished, one of his disciples said to him, 'Lord, teach us to pray, as John taught his disciples.'" (Luke 11:1)

The Lord Jesus prayed alone, although He was surrounded by His disciples. He taught them to pray and prayed for them, but we never read that He had a prayer meeting with them, or that they talked to God in His presence. Even in Gethsemane, where He told them to watch and pray, He then withdrew from them about a stone's throw to pray alone (Luke 22:41). It is also with regard to prayer that the following applies, *"You have **one** teacher, and you are all brothers"* (Mt. 23:8). His relationship with the Father as the only Son is and remains unique (see John 1:14)!

He never prayed to be seen by men. But His prayer life could not remain hidden. This is why it is said, *"Now it happened that as he was praying alone, the disciples were with him"* (Luke 9:18). He wasn't shy, nor was He embarrassed to pray in the presence of others. On the other hand, how difficult it is for many Christians to pray before eating when they know that unbelievers will see them doing so. It must have deeply impressed the disciples to see their Master praying so often. *"Lord, teach us to pray"* is therefore then their prayer (Luke 11:1).

In addition to the so-called 'Lord's prayer,' which we cannot literally adopt for our time, but from which we can derive important principles with regard to our prayers, the Lord Jesus has given us other valuable guidance for our prayer life. Here are a few suggestions to think about:

- Withdraw to be alone with God. Close one door here in order to enter heaven through another—figuratively speaking; *"But when you pray, go into your room and shut the door and pray to your Father who is in secret. And your Father who sees in secret will reward you"* (Mt. 6:6).
- Pray with faith—without doubting—in the firm expectation of receiving something; *"Therefore I tell you, whatever you ask in prayer, believe that you have received it, and it will be yours"* (Mark 11:24).
- Pray with boldness and urgency. Show God that you are serious and that the matter is important to you; *"He said to them, 'Which of you who has a friend will go to him at midnight and say to him, "Friend, lend me three loaves" ... I tell you... knock'"* (Luke 11:5–9)!
- Pray with perseverance and don't give up! Pray until you get an answer; *"He told them a parable to the effect that they ought always to pray and not lose heart"* (Luke 18:1).
- Pray for those who mock you or persecute you in other ways (Gen. 21:9; Gal. 4:29); *"Pray for those who persecute you"* (Mt. 5:44).

- Forgive your neighbor and don't be bitter against him when you go into prayer; *"Whenever you stand praying, forgive, if you have anything against anyone"* (Mark 11:25).

- Pray in the knowledge that God is your Father and that you now have the wonderful privilege of coming before the Father in the name of His Son—with His authorization—to ask Him for something; *"Until now you have asked nothing in my name. Ask, and you will receive, that your joy may be full... for the Father himself loves you"* (John 16:24, 27).

There are excellent books on the subject of prayer that encourage us to pray. But reading books doesn't turn us into praying believers. You can read the best books on the subject of swimming, and yet remain a non-swimmer all your life. You learn to swim in water—you learn to pray on your knees!

> *Is the disciples' prayer request in Luke 11:1 also your earnest prayer? To what extent do you strive to put the teachings about prayer in the Word of God more into practice in your prayer life?*

Notes:

....
....
....
....
....
....
....
....
....
....
....
....
....
....
....
....
....
....
....
....
....
....
....
....
....
....
....
....

The Obedience of Faith and the Glory of God

"Jesus said, 'Take away the stone.' Martha, the sister of the dead man, said to him, 'Lord, by this time there will be an odor, for he has been dead four days.' Jesus said to her, 'Did I not tell you that if you believed you would see the glory of God?' So they took away the stone." (John 11:39–41)

The confidence of faith is the eye through which we can see the glory of God. *"According to your faith be it done to you"* (Mt. 9:29), the Lord Jesus once said to two blind men. As a result their eyes were opened. It is often unbelief that hinders the work of God, as Matthew 13:58 makes clear, *"He did not do many mighty works there, because of their unbelief."* How much of God's glorious activity we could see in everyday life and then experience how He still moves mountains today if we would trust Him more and in a more childlike way (see Mt. 17:20)!

The Son of God knew from the beginning that God would allow the illness of Lazarus to bring His glory to light (John 11:4). He loved this family at Bethany and they loved Him. Paul writes, *"We know that for those who love God all things work together for good"* (Rom. 8:28)—as it was in this case.

Just as He did with Jairus (see Mark 5:36), the Lord also urged Martha to trust Him in this seemingly hopeless situation. After they finally took away the stone from in front of the tomb in the obedience of faith, the Lord Jesus revealed the glory of God. Sometimes we can only see the wonderful action of God when we take that first step in the obedience of faith.

Jairus saw the glory of God because he listened to the words of Jesus, *"Do not fear, only believe"* (Mark 5:36), and continued walking with Him. Peter, in the obedience of faith, first had to row out into the deep in the middle of the day and let down the nets for the catch to see the glory of God (see Luke 5:4–6). Two of Jesus' disciples, in obedient faith, were to go to a village and simply untie a donkey belonging to a stranger, trusting that they would not be bothered if they said, *"The Lord needs them"* (Mt. 21:2–3). Ananias too only saw what the wonderful grace of God can bring about when, after initial hesitation, he sought out in obedience of faith the one who, until then, had persecuted the believers to the point of blood (see Acts 9:17–18).

God wants us to trust Him when He gives us assignments—even if they may not make sense to us at first or we can't foresee what will come out of them. In such situations the Lord Jesus also says to us, *"Did I not tell you that if you believed you would see the glory of God?"* (John 11:40).

> *Is there something in your life that you know you should be doing, but you hesitate because you fear the consequences? What prevents you from 'letting go' and just trusting the Lord 'blindly'? Dare to step out onto the water to experience more of how wonderfully He operates!*

Notes:

....

....

....

....

....

....

....

....

....

....

....

....

....

....

....

....

Praying with Belief

"Jesus lifted up his eyes and said, 'Father, I thank you that you have heard me. I knew that you always hear me, but I said this on account of the people standing around, that they may believe that you sent me.'" (John 11:41–42)

Here we see on the one hand the perfect dependence of Jesus, but on the other hand also His perfect oneness with the Father. Everything that He did, He did without exception in dependence on His Father and in fellowship with Him. His miracles and signs were the works of the Father, which the Father did through Him (see John 14:10).

In this passage we have the second prayer of Jesus, in which we are told the words He addressed to the Father. While in Luke 10:21 (NKJV) He began His prayer with the words, *"I praise you, Father,"* here He first said, *"Father, I thank you."* Obviously, Jesus' prayer life was primarily characterized by praise and thanksgiving!

If we take a closer look at the contents of Paul's prayers, we'll see that for the most part, they consisted of thanksgiving! Therefore, he was able to urge both the Colossians and the Philippians with moral authority not to forget to give thanks when praying (see Col. 4:2; Phil. 4:6). There is much truth in the well-known saying, "Thanksgiving protects from faltering and praise draws us upwards"—but we'll only experience it if we actually practice it!

Here the Lord Jesus thanked for the answer before the answer became apparent. Since He did at all times what was pleasing to God, He had complete assurance that the Father was with Him (see John 8:29). Evidently, He had prayed for the raising of Lazarus at an earlier time—perhaps during the two days He waited before responding to Mary and Martha's cry for help. His prayer showed no vague hope, but rather the firm conviction that He would receive something. To Him, the answer was so certain that He considered it to have already happened. In this, the Lord Jesus again implemented something that He Himself had taught His disciples, *"Therefore I tell you, whatever you ask in prayer, believe that you have received it, and it will be yours"* (Mark 11:24).

In the history of the Church also there have always been believers who, already on their knees in faith, have gained the conviction that God has heard their prayer. It is a great thing when you can already give thanks for the answer, even though it has not yet become visible. The following story from the life of Hudson Taylor illustrates this in an impressive way:

"When the missionary Hudson Taylor was on his first voyage to China, the ship was often hampered in its journey both by a lack of wind and adverse winds. Once, the ship passed an island that was said to be inhabited by cannibals. Just then the wind died down again and the ship slowly drifted toward the fateful coast on the mirror-smooth surface. Horror gripped the travelers on board at the thought of the dreadful welcome that awaited them. In his distress the captain came to the missionary and said, 'You believe that your God answers prayers. Call him! If your prayers don't work, we're lost.'

'I will pray,' Hudson Taylor replied, 'but only on the condition that you have all sails set to catch the wind that God will send.'

The unbelieving captain was afraid of making a fool of himself and didn't want to unfurl the sails in this complete calm. The missionary, however, declared that he wouldn't begin to pray until the captain had demonstrated by his actions, that the boat was ready for when Taylor's prayer was answered. Closer and closer they drifted toward the coast. At last the captain fulfilled the passenger's wish, although not a breeze had yet blown. Hudson Taylor retired to his cabin and laid the collective distress before the Lord. While he was still praying, there was a loud knock at his door. The captain stood outside and shouted, 'Are you still praying for wind? You can stop. We have more than we need.' And so it was. At the moment of greatest danger, when the ship was already very close to land, the wind had risen which drove the vessel back out to sea."[7]

John writes, *"This is the confidence that we have toward him, that if we ask anything according to his will he hears us. And if we know that he hears us in whatever we ask, we know that we have the requests that we have asked of him."* (1 John 5:14–15). What a blessing it is and how strengthening for our faith to be allowed to have such experiences!

Perhaps you're asking yourself how you can come to have the requests on your heart that God will surely answer. David gives us the answer, *"Trust in the LORD, and do good; dwell in the land and befriend faithfulness. Delight yourself in the LORD, and he will give you the desires of your heart."* (Ps. 37:3–4). If you trust Him, live in devotion to Him, and make Him the center of your thinking, the Holy Spirit will form in your heart the requests that come from God. The New Testament says, *"Beloved, if our heart does not condemn us, we have confidence before God; and whatever we ask we receive from him, because we keep his commandments and do what pleases him"* (1 John 3:21–22).

---

7 *Der Herr ist nahe!* CSV-Verlag, Hückeswagen

> *What does it mean to you practically to 'delight yourself in the Lord'? Do you pray expectantly and with a clear conscience? Praise and glorify the Lord when you pray, and don't forget to give thanks!*

Notes:

....
....
....
....
....
....
....
....
....
....
....
....
....
....
....
....
....
....

Answers to Prayer—An Affirmation for Your Service

"Father, I thank you that you have heard me. I knew that you always hear me, but I said this on account of the people standing around, that they may believe that you sent me." (John 11:41–42)

Lazarus' sickness was allowed so that the Son of God would be glorified by it (see John 11:4). The mighty power that was active in raising Lazarus from the dead brought the glory of God to light (see John 11:40). What was God's purpose in this sign and miracle? To make people realize that Jesus Christ is truly the Son of God (see John 20:31).

On another occasion, when the disciples saw their Lord walking on the water and experienced Him coming to their aid in the storm, they bowed down before Him and cried, *"Truly you are the Son of God"* (Mt. 14:33)! God sometimes works miracles, large and small, in our lives too. Why is that? So that we can get a deeper impression of His greatness and worship Him with admiration. When was the last time you did this with your whole heart?

The Son of God had come to reveal the Father and glorify Him before the eyes of men. Because He acted in dependence at Lazarus' grave and prayed audibly, the Father received the glory for the miracle that followed. Knowing that He was at the center of God's will, He magnified

Him Who hears prayer (Ps. 65:2) and focused the attention of all on Him. This should also be our intention when we ask God for something!

Just as the Father sent the Son into this world to glorify Him here, the Son also sent us into this world to magnify Him here (see John 20:21). Disciples of Jesus can be recognized, among other things, by the fact that they cling to His promises with the confidence of faith, keep His commandments and experience how God responds to prayer (see John 15:7–8).

The scene at Lazarus' tomb reminds us in a certain sense of Elijah on Mount Carmel. The prophet there cried out loudly in front of the crowd, *"O LORD, God of Abraham, Isaac, and Israel, let it be known this day that you are God in Israel, and that I am your servant, and that I have done all these things at your word. Answer me, O LORD, answer me, that this people may know that you, O LORD, are God, and that you have turned their hearts back."* (1 Ki. 18:36–37). Elijah prayed for God to confirm his service to Israel in the eyes of the people. Knowing that he was on this mountain at the center of God's will, he could express this request with frankness and boldness. His motive was to glorify God and his prayer was answered.

> How do you, through your prayer life,
> give God the opportunity to show that
> He is still the 'hearer of prayer' (Ps. 65:2)
> today? Do you share your experiences of
> answered prayer with others, so that God
> may be glorified and more people may
> find the courage to trust Him?

Notes:

....

....

....

....

....

....

....

....

....

....

....

....

....

....

....

....

....

The All-Decisive Line of Vision

"Jesus wept... And Jesus lifted up his eyes and said, 'Father, I thank you.'" (John 11:35, 41)

The Man Who sat down tired at the well at Sychar is the same One Who gives us the Holy Spirit so that we can enjoy eternal life (see John 4:14). The Son of the carpenter Who slept on a pillow in the boat, had the power to subdue the storm and the waves and to save His disciples from every danger. He was inwardly moved by the misery of the people and at the same time able to instantaneously heal the sick with one word. He showed both human feelings and divine power. He encouraged the downcast, lifted up tired souls through words of grace, and at the same time raised the dead from the grave. He wept with those who wept and rejoiced with those who rejoiced (see John 12:1–2).

The life of Jesus was marked by an expectant gaze toward heaven. When it came to meeting the needs of 5000 hungry men, He took five loaves of bread and two fish in His hands, looked up and thanked God for them (see Mt. 14:19). Another time He looked up to heaven and sighed while healing a deaf man with a speech impediment (see Mark 7:34). At the tomb of Lazarus, He also looked in the same direction when He prayed with the firm conviction that the Father would hear Him—and again the glory of God shone forth! Finally, a few hours before His death,

He once again raised His eyes upwards with confidence and prayed as no man has ever prayed before (see John 17).

Looking at the consequences of sin brings tears; but looking up leads to gratitude. When tears are accompanied by prayer, sadness does not lead to resignation. Hannah prayed with tears. She poured out her soul before the LORD and took courage. She had come to Shiloh with a broken heart, but she went home with confidence (see 1 Sam. 1:18). God heard her plea because her purpose was the glory of God and her desire to be in accordance with His will.

Neither did Jehoshaphat resign when he found himself with the people in what was, from a human point of view, a hopeless situation. He confessed his helplessness to the LORD in prayer—but he didn't stop there—he prayed, *"We are powerless against this great horde that is coming against us. We do not know what to do, but our eyes are on you"* (2 Chron. 20:12). The Psalmist had the same line of sight and said, *"To you I lift up my eyes, O you who are enthroned in the heavens!"* (Ps. 123:1)! In the New Testament we're called to turn our eyes to *"the founder and perfecter of our faith"* (Heb. 12:2), who is now *"crowned with glory and honor"* (Heb. 2:9), sitting at the right hand of God. A life of dependence is linked to an attitude of anticipation and an unceasing gaze upwards—until He is gracious unto us (see Ps. 123:2).

> *What are your eyes focused on today? Are your eyes fixed on the circumstances, or do you decide to look beyond them at the One Who is above circumstances and to Whom all power is given in heaven and on earth? Be aware that every tear you shed here is recorded by God and at the same time His ears are toward your cry (Ps. 56:8; 34:15)!*

Notes:

....

....

....

....

....

....

....

....

....

....

....

....

....

....

Are You Only Serving, or Are You Also Following?

"If anyone serves me, he must follow me; and where I am, there will my servant be also. If anyone serves me, the Father will honor him." (John 12:26)

There is much service being done today in the name of the Lord Jesus. But how many Christians are there who also deny themselves, take up their cross daily and live in the same spirit of Jesus? Striving for a position in the world and service to the Lord do not go together. The words of Jesus, *"You cannot serve God and money"* (Mt. 6:24), are still very relevant today!

The Lord Jesus made Himself perfectly one with the Father's interests and will on earth. He took God's side so consistently and stood up for His interests, that those who reproached God automatically rejected the Son of God as well (see Rom. 15:3). Today, when someone publicly takes the side of the rejected Christ, breaks his friendship with the world and serves the Lord Jesus, he has the firm promise that the Father will honor him.

But discipleship is also connected with imitation. Disciples of Jesus should reflect the heart of their Lord! What did His attitude of heart look like? As an example, He did not strive to be publicly known. Instead, He washed the dirty feet of His disciples in the upper room with moving humility. When He was attacked or wrongly accused, He didn't defend Himself, but surrendered to the One Who judges justly. He also showed permanent dependence and complete faith in His prayer life.

The reward for faithfulness in service and discipleship is that the servant will live with the Lord Jesus in the Father's house—*"where **I** am"*—for all eternity (see 1 Thess. 5:10; John 14:3). This is the place of eternal joy, where the Son of God has always been and now is as a glorified man (see John 17:24). To be with Him and to see Him—that is what defines heaven!

> *Just one glimpse of Him in glory*
> *will the toils on earth repay.*

In what way do you make God's interests your interests? Are there situations in your life where you can sympathize with something of what is written in Romans 15:3 about the Son of God, "The reproaches of those who reproached you fell on me"? Realize with fresh awareness, that in the Lord's service, it is especially a matter of having the right spirit and attitude of heart!

Notes:

....

....

....

....

....

....

....

....

....

....

....

....

....

....

....

....

....

....

....

....

....

....

....

....

....

....

....

....

....

Honor from God or from Man?

"If anyone serves me, he must follow me; and where I am, there will my servant be also. If anyone serves me, the Father will honor him." (John 12:26)

What kind of honor are you looking for? The glory that comes from God or the glory that people give you? Paul writes, *"If I were still trying to please man, I would not be a servant of Christ."* (Gal. 1:10). The following three statements of Jesus make it clear how important it is to seek the glory that comes from God alone, *"How can **you** believe, when you receive glory from one another and do not seek the glory that comes from the only God? ... The one who speaks on his own authority seeks his own glory; but the one who seeks the glory of him who sent him is true, and in him there is no falsehood ... Yet **I** do not seek my own glory; there is One who seeks it, and he is the judge."* (John 5:44; 7:18; 8:50).

Due to the fact that the Lord Jesus served with this attitude of heart, He experienced the Father honoring Him during His life. Peter writes, *"When he received honor and glory from God the Father, and the voice was borne to him by the Majestic Glory, 'This is my beloved Son, with whom **I** am well pleased'"* (2 Pet. 1:17). But this was only the beginning. After He had returned to heaven, we read in Hebrews 2:9, *"but we see... Jesus... crowned with glory and honor."*

The Father honors those who serve the Son. This is true in the first place with regard to eternity, but certainly also for the time here on earth. It is very remarkable what promises the Lord Jesus gives in the present time to those who give up something for His sake and the sake of the gospel: *"Jesus said, 'Truly, I say to you, there is no one who has left house or brothers or sisters or mother or father or children or lands, for my sake and for the gospel, who will not receive a hundredfold now in this time, houses and brothers and sisters and mothers and children and lands, with persecutions, and in the age to come eternal life.'"* (Mark 10:29–30).

It's not without reason that the 'fathers' are omitted here in the enumeration of the reward. Those who are willing to give the kingdom of God first priority in their lives and to give up things for the sake of the ministry of Jesus, should know that they have a Father in heaven Who knows all their needs, and will supply them (see Mt. 6:32–33)!

The names of some women who served the Lord Jesus with their possessions have been preserved in the Word of God (see Luke 8:1–3). Mary too was prepared to sacrifice something very precious for her Lord. The value of the nard with which she anointed Him was at that time approximately equivalent to the annual salary of a day laborer! What does the Lord say about her? *"She has done what she could"* (Mark 14:8). There is hardly a greater honor that could be given! Then He adds, *"Truly, I say to you, wherever the gospel is proclaimed in the whole world, what she has done will be told in memory of her"* (Mark 14:9). Thus once again God's promise was fulfilled, which is still fully valid in our time, *"those who honor me I will honor"* (1 Sam. 2:30).

> *The Pharisees loved the first seats—the seats of honor—in the synagogues. How can you, in view of your life, protect yourself from such an attitude of heart? Do you believe that God will fulfill the promises of Mark 10:29–30 and Matthew 6:32–33 in your life as well, if you rely on them in faith and act accordingly? The Lord could say of Mary, "She has done what she could." What can He say about your life?*

Notes:

....

....

....

....

....

....

....

....

....

Agony of Soul

"Now is my soul troubled." (John 12:27)

The Son of God had talked with His disciples about the path of discipleship. He spoke to them about the cost, but also about the reward that awaited them. Then suddenly the cross stood before His holy soul. The thought that in a few days, because of the guilt of others, He would be forsaken by God and would have to die, deeply distressed Him. But this was the price He had to pay, so that people could be saved from hell to live together with Him in the Father's house for all eternity.

The Lord Jesus spoke openly in prayer with His Father about how He felt. He did not use any empty platitudes or learned expressions, but said things as they were and how He felt them. Do you do this when you pray? In the Psalms we can often read where the Spirit of God inspired believers to record their feelings in prayers. Our feelings are not irrelevant to God. On the contrary! He is compassionate, gives true comfort, and gives the encouragement we need at the right time.

The Son of God experienced fear and dismay in a much deeper way than we will ever feel. *"In all their affliction he was afflicted"* (Isa. 63:9), Isaiah writes in reference to the Jewish remnant who will one day go through the awful time of the Tribulation. Those in Smyrna who were facing martyrdom, were understood by the Lord Jesus from His own experience (Rev. 2:8–9). He also knows exactly how you feel at this moment!

Jesus was deeply moved in spirit when He saw people crying at the tomb of Lazarus (see John 11:33). He was troubled in spirit when Judas was about to betray Him and shortly afterwards to take his own life (see John 13:21). Now His soul was dismayed because death, the king of terrors, stood before Him (see Job 18:14). Against this background it is touching to read what the Son of God said to His disciples a short time later, *"Let not your hearts be troubled"* (John 14:1). Because He was dismayed and shaken, they no longer needed to be!

We have the firm promise that God will also provide the way of escape out of every temptation, so that we can bear it (see 1 Cor. 10:13). Therefore, we can say with the Psalmist, *"Why are you cast down, O my soul, and why are you in turmoil within me? Hope in God; for I shall again praise him, my salvation"* (Ps. 42:5).

> Do you tell your Lord openly in prayer about your fears and feelings? Are you aware that He can, from His own experience, understand you perfectly? He cares about you (1 Pet. 5:7) and He cares about your feelings!

Notes:

....
....
....
....
....
....
....
....
....
....
....
....
....
....
....
....

Inner Conflict

"Now is my soul troubled. And what shall I say? 'Father, save me from this hour'?" (John 12:27)

The closer the Son of God got to Jerusalem, the greater became the shadow of the cross that fell on His pathway. The sufferings of anticipating what was to happen to Him there at Golgotha increased more and more. On the one hand, He shied away from coming into contact with sin and being forsaken by God, for sin was something foreign to His Being. On the other hand, He wanted to do the will of His Father at all costs—and save us from eternal ruin. In prayer He expresses the inner distress as well as the understandable desire to be saved from this hour. In view of the cross, there was only One Who could truly understand Him—and that was His Father, Who went with Him to Calvary. To Him He turned and opened His heart.

We cannot compare our hardships with what was before the soul of the Son of God on the way to Calvary. Nevertheless, we learn some basic things from the words He said to His Father in prayer.

You may find yourself in situations where you don't know what to pray for. What do you do then? It is precisely in such circumstances that you can pour out your heart to God and tell Him how you feel and what is going on inside you. You may also pray that God will have mercy on you, for example, by releasing you from serious hardships. He doesn't promise to answer your prayer in this way, but He assures you that His peace, which nothing can shake, will then preserve your heart (see Phil. 4:6).

Often God is more glorified when, instead of changing circumstances, He gives us the grace and mercy we need to honor Him in the midst of circumstances through trust and perseverance! Paul pleaded three times at the throne of grace for the Lord to remove the thorn in the flesh that was given to him. But the Son of God was pursuing a higher goal. He explained to His servant that instead of changing the circumstances, He would give sufficient grace for the Apostle to serve Him in weakness (see 2 Cor. 12:9–10). At the throne of grace there is both mercy and grace. God gives both for timely help—for He never arrives too late!

Sometimes we are so overwhelmed by the suffering that sin has brought into this world that we no longer really know what and how to pray. But it is precisely then that the Holy Spirit intercedes for us Himself with groanings too deep for words—and God can understand these sighs perfectly (see Rom. 8:26). Our Lord Himself wept at the tomb of Lazarus and sighed deeply in spirit (see John 11:33). Even if you find yourself in a situation where you are so depressed that you no longer know how to pray, you can still be sure of one thing, *"that for those who love God all things work together for good"* (Rom. 8:28)!

> *When was the last occasion you took the time to really tell God all the issues that are on your mind (see Phil. 4:6), casting all your burdens and worries on Him (see Ps. 55:22; 1 Pet. 5:7)? How often do you pray that God will change circumstances, and how often does He change you through the circumstances? Trust that God, has good intentions with every affliction that He allows and that He will give you all the grace you need to honor Him in difficult trials!*

Notes:

....

....

....

....

....

....

....

....

....

....

My Utmost for His Highest

"For this purpose I have come to this hour. Father, glorify your name." (John 12:27–28)

Despite all the opposition and the anticipation of what awaited Him at Golgotha, the Son of God never lost sight of His mission. On entering this world He said, *"Behold, I have come to do your will"* (Heb. 10:7). Now, some 33 years later, He set His face to go to Jerusalem (see Luke 9:51)—the city *"the city that kills the prophets and stones those who are sent to it"* (Mt. 23:37). Neither the Jews (see John 11:8), nor Herod (see Luke 13:31–32), nor His own disciples could stop Him (see Mt. 16:21–23). His decision was as solid as a rock, *"See, we are going up to Jerusalem, and everything that is written about the Son of Man by the prophets will be accomplished"* (Luke 18:31).

"Father, glorify your name"! What unconditional devotion and consecration to God lie in this prayer! The Son of God had come to glorify His Father through death. He wanted to magnify Him before men and angels—even if the fulfillment of this desire cost Him everything. During His life He said, *"Whoever has seen me has seen the Father"* (John 14:9). But how much God really loves the world, and how just and holy He really is, only became fully evident at the cross. In 6000 years of human history, God has never been glorified as much as through the suffering and death of Jesus on the cross of Calvary!

Just as the light shines brightest in the darkness, God is often most glorified when we trust Him in suffering and persevere in it. We glorify Him in difficult circumstances when we surrender to His will without rebellion, and say "Yes, Father"! God was wonderfully glorified when the other prisoners listened to Paul and Silas, their feet in the stocks, singing praises to Him in the dungeon at Philippi (see Acts 16:25). Peter, like almost all of the twelve apostles, was to glorify his Master in martyrdom (see John 21:19). Stephen glorified the Lord Jesus especially at the very moment when the Jews stoned him—for it was, when facing death, that the life of Jesus shone out from him most brightly (see Acts 7:55–60).

How is God glorified in your life? By making visible in you something of the life or mind of Jesus (see 2 Cor. 4:10). This new life was given to you by God at your conversion. Now it is a matter of living out this life practically! But this will only happen if you realize in faith that you died with Christ to sin, and now let Him live in you in the power of the Holy Spirit (Gal. 2:20). Without death there is no life!

> *"Have this mind among yourselves,*
> *which is yours in Christ Jesus."*
> *(Philippians 2:5)*

> *How do you react when God calls you,*
> *or someone very close to you, to a very*
> *difficult or even 'life-threatening' task?*
> *Could you—in the light of eternity—*
> *even then say soberly, in a balanced way,*
> *"Father, glorify your name"? Paul's pri-*
> *mary concern wasn't to be released from*
> *prison, but rather that Christ should be*
> *magnified in his body, whether by life or*
> *by death (see Phil. 1:20).*
> *Is that your greatest aim too?*

Notes:

....

....

....

....

....

....

....

....

....

....

....

....

....

....

The Response

"'Father, glorify your name.' Then a voice came from heaven: 'I have glorified it, and I will glorify it again.'" (John 12:28)

The prayer of Jesus, *"Father, glorify your name,"* was immediately followed by the response from heaven, *"I have glorified it, and I will glorify it again."* The desire of the Son was so excellent and so pleasing to the Father that He could not keep silent about it.

What is the meaning and significance of these divine words? The works that the Son did in dependence glorified the Father. This was also the case with the raising of Lazarus. Therefore, the Father gave His Son the firm promise that He would answer His request and glorify Himself again. But how was this going to happen? By raising Him from the dead in the power of His own glory (see Rom. 6:4). He did not allow His Holy One to see corruption (see Ps. 16:10)!

The resurrection of the Lord Jesus is of fundamental importance to every believer. Why? First, because it's the divine proof that all our sins are truly atoned for, and second, because His resurrection includes the spiritual raising of all those who believe in Him (see Eph. 2:4–5)! It is not without reason that the Victor of Golgotha—*"the last Adam"* (1 Cor. 15:45)—on the day of His resurrection, immediately went to see His disciples and communicated His resurrection life to them by breathing into them (see John 20:22).

The Lord Jesus said a short, devoted prayer and received a clear answer. We too are not heard for the sake of our many words (see Mt. 6:7), but only because we ask for things in accordance with the will of God. If we make the exaltation of the Father our primary concern, and subjugate our personal wishes to that, all things will be in their proper place. When the Lord Jesus taught His disciples to pray, the first request He presented to them was, *"Our Father in heaven, hallowed be your name"* (Mt. 6:9). When we pray with this attitude, we can trust that we are praying in the name of Jesus—and in this way, He who hears prayer is glorified (see John 14:13; Ps. 65:2).

> *When was the last time you thought about your motivation to pray for something? How dedicated are you in longing for God to be glorified through your life? Remember that prayer is not necessarily about many or beautiful words, but rather about the right attitude and desire of your heart!*

Notes:

....
....
....
....
....
....
....
....
....
....
....
....
....
....
....
....
....
....
....
....
....
....
....
....
....
....
....
....
....

God Still Speaks, Even Today!

"'Father, glorify your name.' Then a voice came from heaven: 'I have glorified it, and I will glorify it again.'" (John 12:28)

Three times the voice of God was heard from heaven when the Lord Jesus was here on earth—and each time the Son of God was praying. The prayer life of Jesus was not a monologue!

He prayed as He was baptized in the Jordan River, surrounded by sinners. Heaven could not keep silent. From the open heaven, the Father testified of His love for the Son and honored Him before all.

Toward the end of His ministry, the Servant of God prayed on the 'Mount of Transfiguration' (see Luke 9:28). He had come as a dependent Man to fulfill the eternal counsel of His Father. Included in these counsels, is that He will one day rule over this earth as King of kings and Lord of lords. Again the voice of God was heard from heaven. There on the mountain He honored the Son of His love in front of the greatest prophets of the Old Testament. They spoke God's words at certain times, but in Him God spoke to His people continually (see Heb. 1:1).

God responds to prayers that are intended to honor Him. In Acts 4 the disciples prayed for boldness to speak the Word of God to the people. God affirmed this prayer and glorified Himself. He gave them boldness to speak freely and gave them great grace so that they could witness with power to the resurrection of Jesus (see Acts 4:31–33). When Peter was in prison, the believers prayed for their brother with one accord and perseverance. This joint striving in prayer was so pleasing to God that He answered that very night. As it is written, *"Before they call **I** will answer; while they are yet speaking **I** will hear."* (Isa. 65:24). Nor could God remain silent when Paul and Silas, with their feet in stocks, called out to Him in prayer in the prison at Philippi, glorifying Him in the ears of the other prisoners by singing His praises (see Acts 16:24–25).

> *When was the last time the Lord spoke directly to you through His Word, through the Holy Spirit or through prophetic ministry? Do you pray for it and then expect Him to do so? Trust that God will glorify Himself if you pray with pure motives for things that are for His glory!*

Notes:

....

....

....

....

....

Learning from the Master

"Take my yoke upon you, and learn from me, for I am gentle and lowly in heart, and you will find rest for your souls. For my yoke is easy, and my burden is light." (Matthew 11:29–30)

Immediately after the Lord Jesus asked His disciples to learn from Him, He presented His thoughts to them. This also applies to prayer; He wants us to imitate Him by praying with the attitude and motivation with which He prayed.

In a nutshell, we can learn the following for our prayer life from the prayers of Jesus in Luke 10, John 11 and John 12:

1. He began His prayer by praising and thanking the Father (Matthew 11:25; John 11:41).
2. In prayer He had the greatness and power of God before His eyes (see Luke 10:21).
3. He prayed in humility and meekness with the will of God in view (see Luke 10:21).
4. He prayed with absolute confidence that the Father would answer His prayer (see John 11:41).
5. He prayed that the Father would affirm His ministry, and at the same time, with the intention that the Father would receive glory for the answering of the prayer (see John 11:42).

6. He spoke with His Father openly about His feelings, and about what moved Him (see John 12:27).
7. He made the glorifying of the Father His highest priority in prayer (see John 12:28).

> *Which of these seven points characterize your prayer life?*

Notes:

....

....

....

....

....

....

....

....

....

....

....

....

....

....

....

....

Thankful to the End

"When the hour came, he reclined at table, and the apostles with him. And he said to them, "I have earnestly desired to eat this Passover with you before I suffer.' ... And he took a cup, and when he had given thanks he said, 'Take this, and divide it among yourselves. For I tell you that from now on I will not drink of the fruit of the vine until the kingdom of God comes.'" (Luke 22:14–15, 17–18)
"As they were eating, he took bread, and after blessing it broke it and gave it to them, and said, 'Take; this is my body.' And he took a cup, and when he had given thanks he gave it to them, and they all drank of it. And he said to them, 'This is my blood of the covenant, which is poured out for many.' (Mark 14:22–24)

When Jesus was 12 years old, He went with His parents to Jerusalem for the Passover. About 21 years later we see Him together with His disciples to eat His last Passover with them. Now the hour had come in which He was to be sacrificed, of Whom the Passover was a fore-shadow: Christ, *"our Passover,"* as the Apostle Paul calls Him in 1 Corinthians 5:7. It was a unique moment when the picture met with its fulfillment!

He had earnestly desired to have fellowship once more with His beloved disciples a few hours before His death. He had told them only a little while beforehand, *"Greater love has no one than this, that someone lay down his life for his friends*" (John 15:13). This death, with all its blessed temporal and eternal consequences, was before Him that evening. He truly loved His own to the very end, that is, to the uttermost!

After they had eaten the last Passover together in the upper room, the Lord instituted the Lord's Supper. During the time of His absence they were to remember what He had done for them out of love—and this still applies to us today!

Three times the Lord Jesus gave thanks in prayer that evening:

- For the cup used at the Jewish Passover, which was symbolic of Israel's deliverance from Egypt.
- For the bread, a symbol of His body, which He gave up to death for believers.
- For the cup, symbolic of His blood, with which He purchased believers, and with which He redeemed them to God.

Although He was about to be led like a lamb to the slaughter, He put Himself entirely into the background, and gave thanks for the mighty blessing that His disciples were to receive through His death.

We are called to give thanks to God in everything (see 1 Thess. 5:18), and even at all times for all things (see Eph.

5:20). How wonderfully the Lord Jesus demonstrated this under the most difficult circumstances.

> *Are you His imitator in this respect too? Is the Lord's Supper (the breaking of bread) just a weekly, obligatory routine for you, or can you say with all your heart, "your name and remembrance are the desire of our soul" (Isa. 26:8)? Realize anew that the Lord longs for you to reflect on His sufferings and proclaim His death!*

Notes:

....
....
....
....
....
....
....
....
....
....
....
....
....

Trust in Self, or Trust in God?

"Simon, Simon, behold, Satan demanded to have you, that he might sift you like wheat, but I have prayed for you that your faith may not fail. And when you have turned again, strengthen your brothers." (Luke 22:31–32)

Here, the Lord called Peter by his old name, Simon, twice. This shows that He was about to tell him something important. There are seven incidents in God's Word in which God called people by their name twice. Each occurrence was a crucial moment in the lives of these people. Sometimes God speaks to us insistently as well, by allowing us to hear a message twice. Do you have an antenna for this?

Four important points can be taken from the Lord's words to Peter:

- He revealed Satan's intention to Peter.
- He told him that He had prayed for him, that his faith would not fail.
- He was sure that His prayer would be answered and that Peter would repent.
- He asked Peter to strengthen his brothers after his restoration.

The Lord Jesus did not 'let Peter play right into Satan's hands.' Before the temptation came, He warned him of the enemy's intentions. In Job we learn that everything that happens in our lives has a prior history in heaven (see Job 1). Nothing happens without God's permission! God is faithful and watches that the enemy does not do anything to us that we cannot bear (see 1 Cor. 10:13)!

Satan's aim was to sift the disciples as wheat is sifted after the harvest—whereby the wheat is sieved for a long time, until all the debris, such as stones, is removed. Satan wanted to really shake their life of faith to see what was left of it. With Peter, he was allowed to do so, because he had to learn an important but painful lesson.

Simon Peter was convinced that he could follow his Master in his own strength. Therefore the Lord had to break his self-confidence in order to be able to use him in ministry later. He did the same with Moses, Jacob, David and Paul, who consequently became useful tools in His hand.

We are very quick to condemn Peter for his self-confidence. But what is actually going on in our own lives? Hardly anyone will freely admit that he thinks he can follow the Lord in his own strength. But in practice, do we not often behave as if we can?

> *In what have you put your trust: in your mind and natural ability or in the power and guidance of the Holy Spirit? How much do you trust in financial security from unjust mammon and how much in God's rock-solid promises? Have you ever asked yourself these questions sincerely before the Lord? David writes in Psalm 62:5, "For God alone, O my soul, wait in silence, for my hope is from him." There is great blessing promised to those who have this attitude!*

Notes:

....

....

....

....

....

....

....

....

....

....

....

....

....

When the Righteous One Prays

"'I have prayed for you that your faith may not fail. And when you have turned again, strengthen your brothers.' Peter said to him, 'Lord, I am ready to go with you both to prison and to death.'" (Luke 22:32–33)

Although the Son of God had expressly warned Peter, he contradicted Him. Only a little while later he denied his Master three times. How did the Lord react to the failure of His disciple? How would we have reacted? Perhaps like this: "I've already told you once, but you wouldn't listen. Now see how you get on!" But that wasn't the mind of Jesus. If He has started a work with us, then He will—despite our failure—also finish it (see Phil. 1:6)!

The Lord did not say here, "I will pray for you," but, "I have prayed for you." His intercession precedes the dangers, storms and trials that we encounter on the way 'home'. James writes, *"The effective, fervent prayer of a righteous man avails much"* (Jas. 5:16 NKJV). How much more does that apply for the prayer of the righteous One! He didn't pray for Peter to be saved from temptation, but that after his fall his faith would not fail. Even if we don't allow ourselves to be helped, and fall because of our failure, He doesn't abandon us; He, the righteous One, then steps in as our Advocate or Intercessor (see 1 John 2:1).

When sin enters our lives, we lose our joy in the Lord and practical fellowship with the Father and the Son. Often the Lord then uses His Word to bring us to self-judgment and confession of our sins (see John 13). God's promise is rock-solid; *"If we confess our sins, he is faithful and just to forgive us our sins and to cleanse us from all unrighteousness"* (1 John 1:9). His goal is for us to be happy Christians who enjoy eternal life to the fullest! Do you?

But the ministry of Jesus as an *Advocate* is not only to convict of sin, but also to reveal the root of sin. He wants to show us how it was possible for us to fall in the first place.

Peter's restoration happened in three steps:

- When Peter had fallen, the Lord looked at him immediately—not reproachfully, but full of gentleness. This look struck Peter right to the heart—for he wept bitterly afterwards (see Luke 22:62). The awareness that the Lord loves us despite our wrong-doing should also break us inwardly and lead us to repentance.
- The Overseer of our souls (see 1 Pet. 2:25) didn't leave Peter alone with his tears. Peter was the first of the disciples whom the Lord sought out after His resurrection to speak with him privately (see Luke 24:34; 1 Cor. 15:5).
- But this wasn't the end of Peter's restoration. In John 21 the Lord Jesus asked him three questions

to make clear to him the root of his failure—his pride and self-confidence. The wonderful thing is that in this conversation the Son of God even enlarged the sphere of ministry of His disciple! Not only was he to be a fisher of men (see Luke 5:10), but also a shepherd, taking care of Jesus' sheep.

The Lord didn't give up on Peter, although He knew that His disciple would fall. Nor will He leave us lying on the ground when we have fallen! *"For the righteous falls seven times and rises again"* (Prov. 24:16). So great is His love for us that He not only died for us, but now too, He is tirelessly working for us from heaven and carrying us on His heart!

> *Why is it so important for you to think about what the Lord Jesus is doing for you now, in heaven, every day? When was the last time you consciously thanked Him for this service? Today, hold your dirty feet out before Him so that He can wash them! David prayed, "Keep back your servant also from presumptuous sins" (Ps. 19:13)! Make that your prayer request too!*

Notes:

....
....
....
....
....
....
....
....
....
....
....
....
....
....
....
....
....
....
....
....
....
....
....
....
....
....
....
....
....

Overcoming Doubts

"I have prayed for you that your faith may not fail. And when you have turned again, strengthen your brothers." (Luke 22:32)

When Peter walked on the water, suddenly doubted and began to sink, the Lord didn't let him drown. At that moment the disciple, in picture, was preserved through faith only because of God's mighty work (see 1 Pet. 1:5).

Now Simon Peter had to re-learn (see Luke 5:8) how profoundly corrupt his natural heart was. This bitter recognition of what he was in himself would test his trust to breaking point. There was a danger that he would despair. The enemy was only waiting for the opportunity to shoot his fiery arrows of doubt to destroy the faith of this fisher of men.

But the Lord gave His disciple courage! *"But I have prayed for you that your faith may not fail."* He had not come to extinguish faintly burning wicks, but to rekindle them (see Isa. 42:3)! We see the wonderful result of His intercession in Acts 2, when Peter, filled with the Holy Spirit, delivered the first Christian message with great boldness before at least 3000 people.

When a believer has sinned, the devil sometimes tries to persuade him that he is not really converted. What can you do when such thoughts arise? We're to take up the shield of faith and stand firm against the enemy in faith (see Eph. 6:16; 1 Pet. 5:9)—by relying on what God tells us in His eternally true word. It also helps to be aware of the following: the *"accuser of our brothers"* (Rev. 12:10) will never persuade an unbeliever that he has not been converted—for he wants to prevent anyone who is not saved from thinking about it! Satan will only cast doubts about salvation on true disciples of Jesus, whom God has chosen in His grace. Paul writes, *"Who shall bring any charge against God's elect? It is God who justifies. Who is to condemn?"* (see Rom. 8:33–34). But the Apostle doesn't stop there. He's completely convinced that neither the present nor the future can separate us from the love of God (see Rom. 8:38–39). This includes our own failures or wrong-doing!

When the Lord Jesus' time here on earth was drawing to a close, He said to His Father with regard to His disciples, *"I kept them in your name, which you have given me. I have guarded them, and not one of them has been lost except the son of destruction"* (John 17:12). He said this, even though He knew that a short time later everyone would leave Him and Peter would deny Him three times. Would it be any different nowadays?

> *Why is it so important for disciples of Jesus to get to know the Lord better on the one hand, and their own hearts on the other? What does it mean to you practically to steadfastly resist Satan in faith? Remember how the Lord Jesus resisted Satan when He was assailed by him in the desert and later in the Garden of Gethsemane!*

Notes:

....
....
....
....
....
....
....
....
....
....
....
....
....
....
....
....

Wanted: Prayer-Warriors!

"Satan demanded... but I have prayed for you." (Luke 22:31–32)

The Son of God knew everything that would happen to Him (see John 18:4). But not only that. He also knew Simon Peter's future. He is the *"God of knowledge"* Who knows everything (see 1 Sam. 2:3)—yet He lived in dependence and prayed for His disciple. Certainly the Lord had already been praying earnestly for Peter and the other disciples the night before He chose His twelve apostles (see Luke 6:12). How many times in the three years when He was with them daily, would He have prayed for them! In John 17, just before His crucifixion, He brings them before His Father again in prayer. He doesn't stop interceding for us as well, until, despite our frequent failures (see James 3:2), we safely reach our destination (see Heb. 7:25; Mt. 14:22–23; Ps. 107:30).

Through prayer, the enemy's purposes are destroyed! Therefore, not only prayer, but also prayer struggle is required for us! Paul writes in connection with the armor of God, *"Praying at all times in the Spirit, with all prayer and supplication"* (Eph. 6:18). Today, brothers and sisters are needed who wrestle and strive for other believers in prayer (see Col. 4:12; Rom. 15:30). This is true for those with whom we have regular fellowship, but also especially for those who have lost their way in the world.

The power of intercession is particularly evident in the example of Paul. After four years of captivity he was still convinced that through the prayers of the Philippians he would be given the grace not to give up in prison, but to continue to honor God through trust (see Phil. 1:18–19)!

Samuel was a prayer-warrior who pleaded much for others. He said to the people of God, who failed again and again, *"Far be it from me that I should sin against the Lord by ceasing to pray for you"* (1 Sam. 12:23). Once he cried out to the Lord all night because Saul had sinned (1 Sam. 15:11). That such prayers are also blessed is made clear by the example of Job. He was given the task of praying for his friends because they had spoken inappropriately of God. God acknowledged this in a wonderful way, for it subsequently says, *"The Lord restored the fortunes of Job, when he had prayed for his friends"* (Job 42:10).

How great is the decline in the people of God today! How should we be acting in light of this? God wants us to step into the breach before Him with Daniel's attitude, or rather to mediate before Him by confessing sins and making intercession (see Dan 9). Moses often did this with great zeal, *"Therefore he said he would destroy them— had not Moses, his chosen one, stood in the breach before him, to turn away his wrath from destroying them."* (Ps. 106:23). *"Then I lay prostrate before the Lord as before, forty days and forty nights. I neither ate bread nor drank water, because of all the sin that you had committed, in doing what was evil in the* sight of the LORD to provoke him to anger. For I was afraid of the anger and hot displeasure that the LORD bore against you, so that he was ready to destroy you. But the LORD listened to me that time also" (Deut. 9:18–19).

Later God had to say, "I sought for a man among them who should build up the wall and stand in the breach before me for the land, that I should not destroy it, but I found none." (Ezek. 22:30). Isaiah writes similarly, "He saw that there was no man, and wondered that there was no one to intercede" (Isa. 59:16). Do these verses still speak to you or have you already given up?

How important is the ministry of intercession! Prayerful intercessors will one day receive a great reward at the judgment seat of Christ—perhaps in some cases much more than those who have served in public. Many today rightly regret the decline of Christianity, but where are those who not only mourn but also devote themselves to the ministry of intercession? God is still searching today for those who humble themselves over the condition of God's people and step into the breach before Him in prayer!

> *Do you believe that the ministry of intercession is valuable in the eyes of God and that He responds in a clear, specific way? Your personal prayer life gives the answer to this question. With more intercession, the Lord would certainly give more vitality again! "If you know these things, blessed are you if you do them"* (John 13:17).

Notes:

....

....

....

....

....

....

....

....

....

....

....

....

....

....

The Unique Prayer

"I am not alone, for the Father is with me... But take heart; I have overcome the world. When Jesus had spoken these words, he lifted up his eyes to heaven, and said, 'Father, the hour has come; glorify your Son that the Son may glorify you.'" (John 16:32–17:1)

The Lord Jesus walked this earth alone and misunderstood. The closer He came to the cross, the lonelier He became. How it must have hurt Him to know that only a few hours before His crucifixion even His closest confidants would abandon Him. But at the same time He rested in the firm assurance that His Father would never leave Him. Because He served Him in unceasing devotion, He always possessed the deep awareness of His presence (see John 8:29).

Twice it is said of Abraham and Isaac, *"They went both of them together"* (Gen. 22:6, 8). David says in Psalm 23:4, *"Even though I walk through the valley of the shadow of death, I will fear no evil, for you are with me."* With this confidence, the Son of God looked up to heaven and spoke with His Father.

What can we learn from this most sublime and unique prayer of Jesus for our prayer life? Just a few brief points:

- The Son of God made the Father's glory His first priority in prayer. He asked for His own glory so that He, from heaven, could glorify the Father. How would He do this? By giving eternal life to those who believe in Him. In this way, Christ, Who is eternal life Himself (see 1 John 5:20), is seen in those who manifest eternal life in their walk. They show something of Him, and this glorifies the Father.

- In His prayer the Lord Jesus spoke about facts. He spoke of the will of the Father and of what He Himself and His disciples had done. We can do that as well. We don't have to think that because God knows everything anyway, we no longer need to tell Him these things. We can thank Him, bring our requests before Him, and talk to Him about all things that concern us.

- Six times He addressed God as Father in this prayer. Once He called Him *"Holy Father"* and once He called Him *"Righteous Father."* God is Father from eternity—a glory that was revealed in a wonderful way only through the coming of the Son of God. The Son lived in the constant enjoyment of this relationship and expressed it also in prayer. Furthermore, He named characteristics of the Father that are connected with the content of His prayer. We can address God in our prayers as He revealed Himself and as it corresponds to our specific prayer requests. Because we are children and sons of God, we can address our Creator as Father—yes, even say *"Abba! Father!"* (Rom. 8:15)! If we feel the need of His grace, we can turn to Him as the *"God of all grace"* (1 Pet. 5:10). When we and others need comfort, we have in Him the *"God of all comfort"* (2 Cor. 1:3, the Greek word can also be translated 'encouragement'). And when we face seemingly insoluble problems, we know Him as the *"Almighty"* for Whom nothing is impossible.

- He asked for preservation, unity and sanctification for His disciples, so that they might enjoy the love of the Father and have His joy within them (see John 17).

Twice we read in the Gospels that the Lord Jesus said, *"I will,"* or *"I desire."* The first time He said it in relation to the cleansing of the leper (see Mark 1:41)—a picture of cleansing or salvation from our sins. In His prayer in John 17 He expressed it in terms of the future of those who are saved. The Hebrew servant said to his Lord, *"I will not go out free"* (Ex. 21:5). In Gethsemane the Lord prayed, *"Not as I will, but as you will"* (Mt. 26:39). But when it came to those whom He bought with His blood, He explicitly spoke of His desire, His will, that they should be with Him to see His glory (see John 17:24).

> *Is it your heart's deep desire that the eternal life you have been given should be visible to the outside world? Do you think about the qualities of God when you talk with Him? In quiet moments, recall to mind the promises of God, Who gives us courage and says, "Behold I am with you always... I will never leave you nor forsake you" (Mt. 28:20; Heb. 13:5)!*

Notes:

....
....
....
....
....
....
....
....
....
....
....
....
....
....
....
....

The Blessing of Good Habits

"He came out and went, as was his custom, to the Mount of Olives... and prayed." (Luke 22:39, 41)

The Lord Jesus cultivated good habits in His life. On the Sabbath He went to the synagogue as was His routine, to read the Word of God with other Jews (see Luke 4:16). When crowds came to Him, it was His custom to teach them (see Mark 10:1). Every morning He took time to let God open His ear in the quiet and be taught by Him (see Isa. 50:4–5). He often stayed on the Mount of Olives to pray there (see Luke 22:39; John 8:1; Luke 21:37–38). It was in this place that He also exhorted the disciples to pray and set a good example for them. How often would He have sought the face of God there!

David too was in the habit of having fellowship with God early in the morning and being before Him in prayer (see Ps. 5:3; 63:1). How important is this quiet time in the morning, about which God's word says, *"From the womb of the morning, the dew of your youth will be yours"* (Ps. 110:3)! But it's also very helpful—if time permits—to have shorter or even longer periods of prayer during the day to keep our fellowship with God fresh and alive. The Psalmist writes, *"Seven times a day I praise you for your righteous rules... At midnight I rise to praise you, because of your righteous rules. Seven times a day I praise you for your righteous rules."* (Ps. 119:164, 62).

Good habits, such as regular early rising, require discipline, determination, and perseverance. The Lord Jesus practiced these things. After caring for people's needs until late at night and bearing their sicknesses and weaknesses (see Mt. 8:17), He nevertheless got up before dawn the next morning to begin the day with prayer in a deserted place (see Mark 1:33–35). Toward the end of His ministry, He was still an 'early riser,' teaching people in the temple early in the morning (see Luke 21:38).

> *How is it that many Christians display impressive discipline in their professional lives, but often let it slip in their spiritual lives? What spiritual habits do you have? Do you look for the "bright morning star" early in the morning?*

Notes:

....

....

....

....

....

....

....

....

....

Force of Habit, or Habitual Determination?

"He came out and went, as was his custom, to the Mount of Olives, and the disciples followed him. And when he came to the place, he said to them, 'Pray that you may not enter into temptation.'" (Luke 22:39–40)

We must be careful that we don't make a law out of a good habit, but remain dependent on God in this regard. For example, the Lord may cause you to be unable to follow a good habit because He has a different plan for you that day. Are you then flexible enough to listen to His voice rather than cling to your habit?

The Lord Jesus was always dependent on His Father even despite His good habits. Normally He taught the crowds that came to Him (see Mark 10:1), but in Mark 1 verses 37–38 He knew that it was His Father's will that day to preach the gospel in other villages. He had been instructed in prayer and put God's personal direction to Him above His good habit!

On the other hand, we shouldn't be tempted by the enemy to give up good habits. The devil will leave no stone unturned to prevent us from going to the place where we usually pray. He did the same with Paul and his companions (see Acts 16:16–17). Daniel was in the habit of getting on his knees three times a day to talk to the living God and praise Him (see Dan 6:10). For this he was threatened and attacked by his adversaries. Nevertheless, he continued faithfully and therefore also experienced how God saved him from the lions' jaws. There is great blessing connected with sticking to good spiritual habits!

As mentioned previously, the Lord Jesus had the habit of going to the synagogue on the Sabbath to read the Word of God with other Jews. The first Christians were accustomed to meeting daily in their houses to break bread. Later we read that on the first day of the week—the Lord's day—the believers met together for the Lord's Supper, i.e. to break bread (see Acts 20:7). We are urged today not to miss gathering as a local assembly, as has unfortunately become a habit for some people (see Heb. 10:25)!

Good spiritual habits must be kept alive, otherwise they risk degenerating into mere formality or religious ritual. In also the meetings for the breaking of bread (the Lord's Supper), the ministry of the word or for prayer, there is the danger that it is not the Holy Spirit but the 'spirit of habit' that determines the course of events!

> *Why is it so important to subject spiritual habits to the guidance of the Holy Spirit? Is it perhaps time for you to re-awaken a good spiritual habit that has fallen asleep? Swim against the tide and hold on to good spiritual habits!*

Notes:

....
....
....
....
....
....
....
....
....
....
....
....
....
....
....
....
....
....
....
....
....
....
....
....
....
....
....
....

The Fiery Darts of the Evil One

"They went to a place called Gethsemane. And he ... began to be greatly distressed and troubled. And he said to them, 'My soul is very sorrowful, even to death... Pray that you may not enter into temptation.' ... He withdrew from them... and knelt down and prayed." (Mark 14:32–34; Luke 22:40–41)

The *"prince of this world"* (John 12:31) was about to load the cannons once again, in order to turn the *"Prince of peace"* (Isa. 9:6) away from the path of obedience. However, he couldn't find any weakness in Him that could offer a point of attack (see John 14:30). From the outset of the Lord's public ministry in the wilderness, Satan, the ancient serpent, had tried to tempt Him. Here in Gethsemane he appeared as a roaring lion, who painted the *"king of terrors"* before His eyes (Job 18:14) and the authority of darkness. He shot fiery arrows at the faithful Servant of God (see Eph. 6:16) to hinder Him from going to Golgotha.

Less than 24 hours later the hands and feet of Jesus were to be driven through with nails into the accursed tree. Darkness, distance from God, and the merciless judgment of Him Who is too pure of eyes to see evil, were before the eyes of His heart at that moment. Fear and dismay overcame Him. How must He, the Holy One Who hates wickedness (see Ps. 45:7), have shrunk from and been revolted by coming into contact with sin; it was even heaped upon Him! He knew the word of the

Psalmist who prophetically wrote about Him on the cross, *"Evils have encompassed me beyond number; my iniquities have overtaken me, and I cannot see; they are more than the hairs of my head; my heart fails me."* (Ps. 40:12).

He withdrew—a stone's throw away. About a thousand years previously, the man after the God's heart (see Acts 13:22) had defeated the giant Goliath in battle with a stone's throw. The *"Lion of the tribe of Judah"* (Rev. 5:5) fought without stone and slingshot however, but with a divine weapon that is powerful to destroy everything that is contrary to the will of God. This time He did not lift up His eyes to heaven, but knelt down, fell to the earth and prayed as no man had ever prayed before!

> *Are you aware that it was also your sins that brought the Son of God into this terrible distress? How does what happened there in Gethsemane affect your attitude toward sin and things that quickly lead you into sin? Thank your Savior for saying to the Father in Gethsemane—and because of His love for you—"Not my will, but yours be done" (Luke 22:42)!*

Notes:

....

....

....

....

....

....

....

....

....

....

....

....

....

....

....

....

....

....

....

....

....

....

....

....

....

....

....

Knowledge of Scripture, without Knowledge of Self?

"When he came to the place, he said to them, 'Pray that you may not enter into temptation.' ... And he came to the disciples and found them sleeping. And he said to Peter, 'So, could you not watch with me one hour? Watch and pray that you may not enter into temptation. The spirit indeed is willing, but the flesh is weak.'" (Luke 22:40; Mt. 26:40–41)

In Gethsemane the Lord Jesus twice urged His disciples to watch and to pray—and each time He Himself set a good example for them. He knew how important prayer is to resist temptation (see Luke 11:2–4). Did He not feel the need to pour out His own heart in prayer before His Father, in the face of the temptation that was coming? How perfectly what He told others corresponded with what He did Himself as a dependent Man (see John 8:25)!

He withdrew from the others and entered into the presence of God. He spent an hour there in earnest prayer. Then He came back to check on His disciples, but instead of praying and staying awake, they slept. He longed for vigilant comforters—but He found none. Even Peter, who had just before claimed in over-confidence that he was prepared even to die with his Master, did not actually manage to watch with Him for one hour.

Again He withdrew for prayer. The idea of soon falling into the hands of the living God, laden with the sin of others, grieved His holy soul until His death. It seems that the Servant of God wrestled in prayer three times that evening, each time for one hour. What an example! His disciples, on the other hand, were asleep each time He came to them. Just a few hours before, He had announced to them that Satan was desiring to sift them all like wheat—and that they would all abandon Him (see Luke 22:31; John 16:32). How much this message alone should have driven them to prayer! But their self-confidence (see Mt. 26:35) and lack of prayer caused them all to fail! When a short time later the temptation came, *"they all left him and fled"* (Mark 14:50).

William Kelly writes compellingly, "There is nothing that so tends, where it is severed from Christ, to destroy dependence, as a large knowledge of the word of God. And that is where our danger lies. The greater our knowledge of the word of God, where it is separated from the sense of utter weakness, and consequently from the need of watching and praying, the greater the danger. This is a solemn warning for our souls. There is no doubt plenty of knowledge of Scripture, and of what is called intelligence of truth; but do our souls keep up this sense of our need and weakness, and the expression of it to God? 'Watch and pray, lest ye enter into temptation.'"[8]

---

8   *The Bible Treasury, New Series*, 1911, p. 204

The awareness of our own weakness—if it is real—will lead us to watch and pray. But if we only talk about our weak state without at the same time practically realizing our dependence, then this is basically nothing but pious hypocrisy. Prayer is the best medicine against spiritual weakness. Only repentance and a sincere confession will help against lukewarmness and indifference!

> *What are you doing to ensure that your knowledge of Scripture is and remains paired with a real awareness of your weakness and an active dependency? When was the last time you watched "one hour" in prayer and actively practiced your dependence in this way? Pray that God will help you to become more like your Example in this respect!*

Notes:

....

....

....

....

....

....

....

....

Vigilance in Prayer

"Watch therefore, and pray always." (Luke 21:36 NKJV)

After the Son of God had opened His disciples' hearts a little, He said, *"Remain here, and watch with me"* (Mt. 26:38). He asked them to watch with Him, but not to pray for Him. In this terrible hour, His human heart yearned for sympathy. But how could a man intercede for Him before God? He had to fight this battle alone on His knees, and for this very reason He distanced Himself from His closest familiar friends. If He, the only sinless Man, felt so much the need for prayer in the hour of temptation, how much greater should our longing be!

What does it actually mean to watch? First of all, watching is the opposite of sleeping. When someone is asleep, he's no longer aware of reality around him and is accordingly not prepared when the enemy attacks. A Christian who is not vigilant has no vital fellowship with his Lord, and thus becomes a target of the enemy and oversleeps opportunities for service that the Lord gives him. Watchfulness, on the other hand, means involving the Lord in all the circumstances of daily life, always placing Him before us (see Ps. 16:8), and never letting the ties of communion be broken. If we're vigilant, everything transforms into prayer! The Lord Himself had said to His disciples, *"Watch therefore, and pray always"* (Luke 21:36 NKJV). By being vigilant, we recognize, so to speak,

Satan's fishhook under the worm, because the spiritual man discerns all things (see 1 Cor. 2:15)!

Twice the wisest man in the world writes, *"A little sleep, a little slumber, a little folding of the hands to rest, and poverty will come upon you like a robber, and want like an armed man."* (Prov. 6:10–11; 24:33–34). How much better it is to fold your hands in prayer instead! But we must also be careful that prayer does not degenerate into a mere duty or a ritual. How quickly it can happen that we fall asleep in prayer, for example, by starting to become formal or by lecturing God! It is His wish that we pray specifically, trustingly and with grateful hearts! Paul writes, *"Continue steadfastly in prayer, being watchful in it with thanksgiving."* (Col. 4:2).

Peter didn't take to heart the Lord's admonition to watch and pray. It is therefore no wonder that he fled a short time later when the soldiers came. But not only that: without having prayed, he put himself in great danger and followed John into the courtyard of the high priest. When a short time later the rooster crowed twice, Peter had already denied his Lord three times. GT Bull said the following catchy phrase about this situation, "We should think on the 'stone's throw', lest we will weep at the cock's crow."[9]

---

9   GT Bull, *The Anguish In The Grass, Learning to pray with Jesus*, Hodder and Stoughton, 1975, p. 127

But Peter learned from his mistakes! That's why he was also empowered by God to warn others not to make the same mistakes. With a shepherd's heart he admonishes the faithful, *"Be sober-minded; be watchful. Your adversary the devil prowls around like a roaring lion, seeking someone to devour"* (1 Pet. 5:8). Instead of sleeping like the ten virgins, the Apostle now lived in the light of eternity, for he writes, *"The end of all things is at hand; therefore be self-controlled and sober-minded for the sake of your prayers"* (1 Pet. 4:7).

> *In what way can you see a connection between lack of prayer and spiritual failure in your life? How easy it is for us to stay up late at the weekend, to talk or to surf the internet unnecessarily! But how difficult it is for us to spend an hour in the evening, either alone or with others, in prayer! What is the reason for this and how can you change this for yourself?*

Notes:

....
....
....
....
....
....

Outward Position for Prayer—More for Appearance Than a Deliberate Choice?

"He... knelt down... fell on the ground... on his face and prayed."
(Luke 22:41; Mark 14:35; Mt. 26:39)

At this point the position the Lord Jesus took in prayer is mentioned for the first time—He knelt down. In this way He took the external attitude that marked Him inwardly—dependence and submissiveness. Even in this dark hour, He honored His Father through His humility in prayer.

The heaviness of what was before Him made Him sink to the ground. His holy face, which had shone in glory on the mountain a short time before, now touched the dust of the cursed ground. Only a few hours later He was to lie in the dust of death (see Ps. 22:15). But on this mountain, where once He knelt down and lay on His face in fear and dismay, His feet will one day stand when He appears in great power and glory (see Zech. 14:4)!

The Word of God shows us that men of God prayed in different positions. Abraham stood before the Lord as he wrestled with God for the righteous in Sodom (see Gen. 18:22). Moses prostrated himself before Him when the people failed terribly (see Deut. 9:18). David sat before the Lord to speak to Him after receiving a prophetic message from Nathan (see 2 Sam. 7:18). Solomon knelt and stretched out his hands to heaven as he prayed at the dedication of the temple (see 1 Ki. 8:54). Ezra also prayed in this way as he humbled himself with others about the failure of God's people (see Ezra 9:5). Elijah bowed down to the earth and put his face between his knees as he pleaded seven times for God to give rain again after more than three years (see 1 Ki. 18:42). Daniel was in the habit of bowing his knees before God in prayer three times a day (see Dan. 6:10). We also often read about Paul kneeling in prayer (see Acts 20:36; 21:5; Eph. 3:14).

It is interesting and insightful that we repeatedly find people in the Bible kneeling in prayer. We think especially of our Lord in Gethsemane (see Luke 22:41). Through this attitude we express both our submissiveness and our dependence. Over the centuries how many victories have men and women of God won on their knees!

But we shouldn't make unwritten laws, even in terms of our position for prayer. In addition to prayer in the chamber, for example, it's always a blessing to talk to God while walking or driving a car—and experience shows that it is an advantage to keep your eyes open!

"Kneeling down on the beach, we prayed."
(Acts 21:5)

> *Do you kneel in prayer because you have always done so, or do you consciously take this posture to express that you're dependent on God and subordinate to His will? What can you do to ensure that your prayer life doesn't become a mere obligation of duty? In everyday life, use the opportunities that God gives you to talk with Him again and again, even in between regular prayer times!*

Notes:

....

....

....

....

....

....

....

....

....

....

....

....

....

....

The Position of the Praying One—It Can't Get Any Closer Than That!

"He said, 'Abba, Father." (Mark 14:36)

In Gethsemane the Lord Jesus didn't call God the *"Lord of heaven and of earth"* (Mt. 11:25) but addressed Him as *"Father," "my Father,"* and *"Abba, Father."* Even in those moments when He threw Himself to the ground under the mighty shadow of the cross, He lived very consciously in the intimate relationship He had as a Son with the Father. There was no distance or formal restraint with Him. Instead, the words *"Abba, Father"* reveal His complete trust and deep affection for Him Who went to Calvary with Him (see Gen. 22:6).

The word *"Abba"* is of Aramaic origin and was originally a word with which children in the close family circle addressed their father. Later it was used by grown children as a reverent form of address to old men. However, the focus is not only on respect, but also on trust. In the New Testament it occurs only twice in addition to the passage in Mark's Gospel—and both times it illustrates the wonderful relationship and position we have received as children and sons of God (see Rom. 8:15; Gal. 4:6).

To say *"Abba, Father"* to God was outrageous and completely unthinkable for the Jews at that time. Since the Israelites were enslaved under the Law, they feared God.

We, on the other hand, in the freedom of sons of God, can enter into the presence of the Father with confidence and openness (see Eph. 2:18). The Lord Jesus said to His disciples, *"The Father himself loves you"* (John 16:27), and thus He encouraged them to turn directly to Him in prayer.

We have the tremendous privilege to address the Father in the same way that the Son addressed Him—in the most intimate manner! No one else has the right to speak to God in such a close and familiar way as those whom the Father loves with the same love with which He loves the Son (see John 17:23, 26)! The greater the need, the more important it is that we live consciously in the relationship to which the *"God of all grace"* (1 Pet. 5:10) has brought us.

> *How would you describe your relationship with the Father? What are the particular effects that the awareness of this relationship and position have on your prayer life? Today, consciously, seek fellowship with the Father and the Son, and savor the joy that is connected with this (see 1 John 1:3–4)!*

Notes:

....

....

....

....

....

....

....

....

....

....

....

....

....

....

....

....

....

....

....

....

....

....

....

....

....

....

....

....

Trusting God in Difficult Times

"He said, 'Abba, Father, all things are possible for you.'" (Mark 14:36)

"All things are possible with God" (Mark 10:27). With this conviction the Lord told His disciples that the grace of God can save even a rich man—which is completely impossible from a human perspective. In Gethsemane He prayed, *"Abba, Father, all things are possible for you."* His trust in the love of the Father and in His omnipotence remained unbroken to the end of His life.

He knew that with just one request, the Father would have instantly provided Him with more than twelve legions of angels (see Mt. 26:53). In the blink of an eye His enemies would have been destroyed. But because He yielded Himself in submission to the Father's will, the Father sent an angel to strengthen Him during His battle in prayer. Isaiah had written, *"Behold my servant, whom I uphold"* (Isa. 42:1)—and this is exactly what was fulfilled in Gethsemane.

Perhaps you are dejected, discouraged and in danger of giving up. Do not give up! The Son of God not only said, *"all things are possible with God"* (Mark 10:27), but also, *"All things are possible for one who believes"* (Mark 9:23)!

Faith is the invisible hand that touches the Almighty and moves His arm. Through faith the lion's mouth was closed and the power of fire was extinguished. Foreign armies were driven back, the dead were raised and the walls of Jericho were destroyed. Relying on Him, men and women of God over the millennia have time and again received strength in weakness and have become strong in battle (see Heb. 11:30–35). Therefore, the same applies to you today: *Do not fear, only believe*" (Mark 5:36)!

> *Are you aware that the faith that is tested through trials honors God and is much more valuable to Him than all the gold in the world (see 1 Pet. 1:6–7)? "Behold, we consider those blessed who remained steadfast" (Jas. 5:11)!*

Notes:

....
....
....
....
....
....
....
....
....

Striving in Prayer

"In the days of his flesh, Jesus offered up prayers and supplications, with loud cries and tears, to him who was able to save him from death, and he was heard because of his reverence. Although he was a son, he learned obedience through what he suffered." (Hebrews 5:7–8)

The Son of God, to Whom everything has been subject from eternity, has learned by his own experience what it means to obey someone else. His obedience to the Father led to more and more resistance on the part of men and therefore also to suffering in this world. Interestingly, the writer of the letter to the Hebrews makes the statement above in the context of what happened in Gethsemane. Why does he do this? Because it's there that it becomes most clear how far Jesus' obedience went and how difficult it was for Him to endure the sufferings of the cross!

Because of his disobedience, the 'first Adam' was told in the Garden of Eden, *"By the sweat of your face you shall eat bread, till you return to the ground"* (Gen. 3:19). In Gethsemane the *"last Adam"* (1 Cor. 15:45) lay on His face on the cursed ground—because of His unwavering obedience. The idea that He was to be made sin only a few hours later literally forced sweat onto His forehead, which fell as large drops of blood to the earth (see Luke 22:44).

It's moving to see the emotion and intensity with which the Lord prayed in Gethsemane. We read of supplications, pleading, tears, strong crying, a fierce battle and fervent prayer, so intense that His sweat became as great drops of blood that fell on the earth. This goes far beyond anything we're told about the greatest prayers of the Old and New Testaments. Yes, He is the only perfect One!

The Son of God prayed in all the circumstances of His life; but the greater the need became, the more intensely He wrestled in prayer. How often do we behave in exactly the opposite way; difficulties and worries often cause our thoughts to be so strongly absorbed by the problems that we lose sight of God. Yet the trials and tribulations we experience should actually drive us straight into the wide-open arms of God! God encourages us to this end and says, *"Call upon me in the day of trouble; I will deliver you, and you shall glorify me.""* (Ps. 50:15)!

"In you my soul takes refuge;
in the shadow of your wings I will take refuge,
till the storms of destruction pass by."
(Psalm 57:1)

> How do you usually handle it when you are overwhelmed by difficulties? When was the last time you consciously took the time to express your distress, perhaps even with tears and with intense requests before the Lord? If you experience resistance and hostility because of your obedience in faith, remember that the Lord Jesus can understand and empathize with you fully!

Notes:

....
....
....
....
....
....
....
....
....
....
....
....
....
....

Pray, until You Pray!

"So, leaving them again, he went away and prayed for the third time, saying the same words again." (Matthew 26:44)

Three times the Son of God prayed in the Garden of Gethsemane, each time for one hour. With a sense of utmost urgency He repeatedly brought His requests before the Father. Wouldn't five minutes have been enough? No! He needed time to pour out His heart before God until He was at rest on His knees.

That He said the same thing in each of the prayers certainly does not mean He used a literal repetition of every phrase. It means that with fervor and intensity He repeatedly laid out the same requests before the Father. In His first prayer He said, *"My Father, if it be possible, let this cup pass from me; nevertheless, not as I will, but as you will."* The second time He prayed, *"My Father, if this cannot pass unless I drink it, your will be done."* The third time He spoke *"the same words again"* (Mt. 26:39, 42, 44).

When you begin to pray for something, do not give up until you receive it or until God makes it clear to you that it's not His will to give it to you. Pray so long and so intensely until your faith gives you the assurance that you're not talking to yourself, but that your prayer has truly traveled beyond the ceiling and arrived before the throne of grace.

CH Spurgeon writes, "Do not try to put two arrows on the string at once, they will both miss. He that would load his gun with two charges cannot expect to be successful. Discharge one shot first, and then load again. Plead once with God and prevail, and then plead again. Get the first mercy, and then go again for the second. Do not be satisfied with running the colors of your prayers into one another, till there is no picture to look at but just a huge daub, a smear of colors badly laid on."[10]

Of course, it is also good to bring several requests before the Lord while praying, casting all our worries on Him and pouring out our hearts to Him (see Phil. 4:6; 1 Pet. 5:7). But we must be careful that we do not simply chant the requests just to pray dutifully. Isn't it often the case that just a few minutes after getting on our knees, we no longer really know what we have been praying for? God rejoices when we pray boldly and with expectancy!

---

10 *New Park Street Pulpit*, Vol. 6, 1860

> *Is it perhaps time for you to reconsider and possibly correct your prayer habits? Is there something you want to plead for intensely until God gives you the awareness that the prayer has been answered, or He makes you calm about the fact that it is not His will? "Let us approach therefore with boldness to the throne of grace" (Heb. 4:16)!*

Notes:

....

....

....

....

....

....

....

....

....

....

....

....

....

....

....

Dependence, Also in the 'What' and the 'How'

"Yet not what I will, but what you will... not as I will, but as you will." (Mark 14:36; Matthew 26:39)

It's very interesting to see exactly what the Lord Jesus prayed for, and with what inner attitude He did it. On one occasion He said, "what you want" and another time, "as you want." He submitted Himself to the will of God not only in terms of the 'what' but also in terms of the 'how.' He was, for example, not only willing to die, but also to be crucified with all the cruelty that entailed.

We should be dependent on God both in terms of the 'what' and in terms of the 'how.' This means that we not only ask what He wants from us, but also how we should do it. The world says, "The end justifies the means." But the Word of God says, *"An athlete is not crowned unless he competes according to the rules."* (2 Tim. 2:5).

We can also apply the 'how' to the motivation and attitude with which we do something for God. If love for Christ is not the motive for my actions, then even the greatest sacrifice has no value in the eyes of God (see 1 Cor. 13:3)! How much reward is lost in view of the judgment seat of Christ, because we do something with a wrong motive! It is basically very good to give financially, to pray and also to fast—but the Lord makes clear to His disciples how important it is to do these things with the right motives (see Mt. 6:1–18).

> *Perhaps the Lord has already made clear to you the sphere of your service for Him. Do you then also ask Him to show you anew how you are to do this service: i.e. in what way, with what means and at what time? How can you protect yourself from undertaking a task out of a wrong motive?*

Notes:

....

....

....

....

....

....

....

....

....

....

....

....

....

Victory on Your Knees

"Not my will, but yours, be done." (Luke 22:42)

The words, *"not my will, but yours, be done,"* show us the victory that the Son of God won on His knees. He accepted what His Father gave Him—as difficult as it was. This is true victory, through which the devil is put to flight!

This also applies in our lives. Victory doesn't always mean that we get what we ask for, but victory does mean that we submit to the will of God without bitterness in our hearts and say 'yes' to His ways. Charles Stanley aptly said in this regard, "Fight all your battles on your knees and you will win every time."

Three times Paul pleaded fervently that the Lord would remove the thorn from his flesh (see 2 Cor. 12:8). But his prayer was not answered. Instead the Lord wanted to give him something better: Grace, that was sufficient for every situation, enabled him to serve in the power of God and thereby glorify Him. Paul also won the victory on his knees, for he could then say, *"Therefore I will boast all the more gladly of my weaknesses"* (2 Cor. 12:9). Circumstances remained the same, but the Apostle had now received peace in the ways of God, and he leaned in faith on His promise—and that changed everything for him!

> *As a rule, do you usually pray only to get your way, or are you also willing, there on your knees, to allow yourself to be changed and redirected? When was the last time you consciously let go and said, "Not my will, but your will be done"? Trust that God's intentions for you are only good—even if it is through suffering. His thoughts are higher than your thoughts!*

Notes:

....

....

....

....

....

....

....

....

....

....

....

....

....

....

God Can!

"Him who was able to save him from death." (Hebrews 5:7)

The Lord Jesus prayed to Him Who is able to do great miracles! Way back in the Old Testament God had announced that He would raise Christ from the dead. Now the Servant of God demanded the fulfillment of this promise on His knees. He had the confidence that God would actually be able to do what He had promised!

With boldness and certainty the "Founder of our faith" said, *"You will not abandon my soul to Sheol, or let your holy one see corruption. You make known to me the path of life"* (Ps. 16:10–11). Living faith is characterized by a 'firm conviction and fulfillment of that which is hoped for' (see Heb. 11:1)!

Abraham believed God Who raises the dead and *"calls into existence the things that do not exist"* (Rom. 4:17). What was the basis for his faith? He leaned on the word of God with all his heart. Contrary to all human hope, he trusted God—and that is exactly how he honored Him. Why? Because he was fully confident that God is able to do what He promised to do (see Rom. 4:17–20)!

With David we see the same principle. When he received a promise from God, he relied on it in faith and asked God for its speedy fulfillment (see 2 Sam. 7:25–29).

> *Do you do that too? Do you remind God in prayer of what He has promised and ask that He fulfill it? To some this may sound a little disrespectful, but it's exactly this faith that God rejoices in! Because by praying on our knees and giving thanks that God is keeping His promise, we show Him that we really take Him at His word! Faith says, "I know that you can do all things, and that no purpose of yours can be thwarted" (Job 42:2).*

Notes:

....

....

....

....

....

....

....

....

....

....

....

....

....

Upright Life and Answered Prayer

"He was heard because of his reverence." (Hebrews 5:7)

Did the Father answer the pleading of the Lord Jesus in Gethsemane and later at Calvary? God did not spare Him the cup of the God's wrath. On the cross the God's judgment fell upon Him in full force. But in view of His resurrection, God heard Him (see Heb. 5:7).

David writes prophetically of Him, *"He asked life of you; you gave it to him, length of days forever and ever"* (Ps. 21:4). In the prophet Isaiah, God Himself says in view of the resurrection of Jesus, *"In a time of favor I have answered you"* (Isa. 49:8).

The Son of God lived a life of devotion, dependence and reverence toward God. Therefore, He could also say with certainty, *"You will not... let your holy one see corruption"* (Ps. 16:10). Scripture confirms that He was *"heard because of his reverence"* (Heb. 5:7).

Throughout His entire life, the Lord Jesus had the full assurance that the Father was always with Him and always heard Him (see John 11:42). Why was this? Because He was without sin and always did that which honored the Father and pleased Him (John 8:29). John writes in regard to us, *"Beloved, if our heart does not condemn us, we have confidence before God; and whatever we ask we receive from* him, *because we keep his commandments and do what pleases him.*" (1 John 3:21–22).

We see in several places that our lives and God's response to prayer are closely related. Because the Son of God had a pure heart, He could pray with boldness and assurance. He was saved from the mouth of the lion and heard from the horns of the wild oxen (see Ps. 22:21). From Daniel, the faithful man of prayer, we read that he was saved from the lions because He trusted in God and did no wrong (see Dan 6:22–23).

> *Do you tolerate things in your life that burden your conscience? Is there perhaps something that could prevent God from answering your prayers? The author of the letter to the Hebrews could say, "Pray for us, for we are sure that we have a clear conscience, desiring to act honorably in all things." (Heb. 13:18). Does this also apply to your life?*

Notes:

....

....

....

....

Peace in the Storm—How to Become an Overcomer

"Jesus, knowing all that would happen to him, came forward and said to them, 'Whom do you seek?... I told you that I am He. So, if you seek me, let these men go... shall I not drink the cup that the Father has given me?'" (John 18:4, 8, 11)

The Son of God had often said to His disciples that people would mistreat and crucify Him. Now the time that this would be fulfilled had come. It's truly impressive to see the peace He radiated in that moment when He was delivered up and taken captive. With great dignity He faced Judas, the soldiers, the crowds and the chief priests! What majesty and what holy courage, combined with simple dependence on His Father in heaven!

How was this possible? How do you explain the great contrast with the scene in Gethsemane, where only a few minutes before, He had been lying on His face, deeply depressed and in anguish, with great crying and tears? The secret of our peace and spiritual strength also lies in the answer to this question.

Before the temptation came He was in fellowship with His Father. There, in His spirit He was praying through everything that stood before Him like a huge mountain. When the time came, He was completely prepared for it. The temptation had no power over Him, for the peace of

God, which surpasses all understanding, guarded His heart (see Phil. 4:7).

What a contrast to Peter, who slept instead of praying! When the soldiers suddenly came, he drew his sword and tried to confront them with fleshly means. How often do we behave in exactly the same way!

The Lord, on the other hand, had already in Gethsemane in prayer accepted the cup from the Father's hand. Now He didn't defend Himself because He saw the hand of God in the circumstances. On the contrary: He overcame evil with good and healed the severed ear of His enemy (see Luke 22:51). Finally, He went out as the great Overcomer, *"bearing his own cross, to the place called The Place of a Skull... there they crucified him"* (John 19:17–18). He has truly overcome the world (see John 16:33)!

"My peace I give to you."
(John 14:27)

> *What do you do when you realize that trial or temptation is coming your way? Do you look for a way to withdraw and spread it out before the Lord in quietness? If you first talk about the temptation in fellowship with God in prayer, God will also give you the awareness that He is with you when the tempest comes! This also applies to the "little things" of everyday life. "Cast your burden on the LORD, and he will sustain you; he will never permit the righteous to be moved" (Ps. 55:22).*

Notes:

....

....

....

....

....

....

....

....

....

....

....

Wanted: Role Models!

"Jesus said, 'Father, forgive them, for they know not what they do.'" (Luke 23:34)

Of the seven statements of the Son of God on the cross, three of them were prayers. At the beginning, in the middle and at the end He prayed!

Samson, shortly before his death, used his great power, given to him by God, one last time to take revenge on his enemies. The Son of God, however, showed the power of His love by praying for the forgiveness of His enemies. When man's sin reached its peak, the Savior's love shone forth most brightly! Paul writes, *"Love... is not irritable... [it] endures all things"* (1 Cor. 13:4–7).

The Master had told his disciples, *"Love your enemies and pray for those who persecute you"* (Mt. 5:44). Under the most difficult circumstances He implemented what He Himself had preached—for He not only taught the truth, but He lived it out constantly (see Acts 1:1). John writes, *"Grace and truth subsists through Jesus Christ"* (John 1:17 JND).

Stephen obviously took the example of his Lord to heart. Only a few seconds before he collapsed and died under the stones thrown by the Jews, he prayed that this sin would not be attributed to them (see Acts 7:60). But there was this difference to the prayer of his Master—

Stephen prayed for himself first (see Acts 7:59) and only afterwards for his enemies. With the Lord Jesus it was the other way round. *"That in everything **he** might be preeminent"* (Col. 1:18)!

> *Do you pray for people who insult you or openly attack you? In what ways do you strive to become more like the Lord Jesus in this respect, and thereby be an example to others? Solomon writes, "Draw me after you; let us run" (SoS. 1:4). Words teach—role models inspire!*

Notes:

....

....

....

....

....

....

....

....

....

....

....

....

Serving in Prayer

"Jesus said, 'Father, forgive them, for they know not what they do.'" (Luke 23:34)

When the Lord Jesus hung on the cross, His pierced hands could no longer serve the sick—humanly speaking. His feet, pierced with nails, were no longer able to walk through cities and villages to proclaim the Gospel of the kingdom. Even His disciples, who had all fled, He could no longer teach.

Was there nothing He could do in these terrible hours to be a blessing to the people? Yes, He could pray—and that is exactly what He did! When He hung there between heaven and earth, He made *"intercession for the transgressors"* (Isa. 53:12). An important lesson for each of us!

The example of the Lord Jesus also encourages us to pray for those who, humanly speaking, it seems impossible will be saved. Who among us, in this situation, would have prayed in faith for these murderers? But didn't this very prayer of the Son of God contribute to the fact that about 50 days later 3000 people were converted all at one time?

Who prayed for the greatest of sinners—the one who persecuted the assembly of God to the point of blood, had the believers thrown into prisons and forced the disciples to blaspheme the name of their Master? Stephen! How did God answer this? He made the former blasphemer, persecutor and insolent opponent (see 1 Tim. 1:13) into a servant of the gospel and the assembly of God (see Col. 1:23, 25). The grace of God used this man to write 14 letters of the New Testament and to work more than all the other apostles (see 1 Cor. 15:10)!

Are you currently unable to be active in a particular work for the Lord that you would like to do because of illness or other circumstances? Perhaps God has taken you aside so that you can spend more time in prayer in the important ministry of intercession.

> *Don't give up praying for people among your acquaintances where it seems completely hopeless that they will yet be converted. "With man it is impossible, but not with God. For all things are possible with God" (Mark 10:27)!*

Notes:

....
....
....
....
....

The Power of Love

"About the ninth hour Jesus cried out with a loud voice, saying, 'Eli, Eli, lema sabachthani?' that is, 'My God, my God, why have you forsaken me?'" (Matthew 27:46)

The crucifixion of the Lord of glory was by far the most extraordinary event that has ever taken place here on earth. Even the desperate cry, *"My God, my God, why have you forsaken me?"* is unique in the history of mankind. David writes, *"I have been young, and now am old, yet I have not seen the righteous forsaken"* (Ps. 37:25). But about a 1000 years later it happened: The righteous Man was forsaken by God—and that because of my sins and yours! *"Christ also suffered once for sins, the righteous for the unrighteous... He himself bore our sins in his body on the tree"* (1 Pet. 3:18; 2:24).

From Bethlehem to Calvary, He lived a unique life to the glory of God. When He prayed at the beginning of His public ministry, the heavens opened and God publicly testified of the delight He took in the life of His Son. But now, as He hung from the cursed tree lifted up above the earth, heaven remained closed despite His calling. He had said to the Jews with peace in His heart, *"He who sent me is with me. He has not left me alone"* (John 8:29). But now He cried out in terrible agony, asking, *"My God, my God, why have you forsaken me?"*

To this mighty question the heart of the believer answers, "For my sake!" There is probably nothing that sanctifies the soul as much as contemplating this scene at Calvary. What kept the Son of God hanging there on the cross? Love for His Father and love for you and me! He had said to His disciples, *"I do as the Father has commanded me, so that the world may know that I love the Father"* (John 14:31). And every child of God can add: He *"loved me and gave himself for me"* (Gal. 2:20). Solomon writes, *"Many waters cannot quench love, neither can floods drown it"* (SoS 8:7).

> *When was the last time you expressed worship to the Son of God for this love? What happens in your heart when you reflect on the three hours of darkness? Give Him an answer through your life to what He did for you on the cross!*

Notes:

....

....

....

....

....

....

....

....

Unshakable Trust

"My God, my God, why have you forsaken me?... Yet you are holy, enthroned on the praises of Israel." (Psalm 22:1, 3)

Since childhood, the Lord Jesus suffered because of the rejection and sinful behavior of men. Satan's temptation, to which He was exposed especially at the beginning of His public ministry, added to His suffering. But all this cannot be compared with the three hours of darkness when He, the Holy One, burdened with innumerable sins, fell into the hands of the living God.

What were His thoughts focused on in those terrible moments? He prayed, *"Yet you are holy, enthroned on the praises of Israel"* (Ps. 22:3). With Him, the perfect One, no rebellious thought could ever arise. On the contrary: He acknowledged the holiness of God and justified Him in His anger over sin. He was willing to suffer to magnify the holiness of God, and so that His redeemed heavenly people could sing His praises!

From the manger to the cross, the Son of Man was cast upon God (see Ps. 22:10). He trusted Him during His life, in view of His resurrection, and even when He was bearing the judgment of God! During the first three hours on the cross, His enemies cried out, *"He trusts in God; let God deliver him now, if he desires him"* (Mt. 27:43). But although there was no instant deliverance, He continued to trust and said, *"On you was I cast from my birth, and from my mother's womb you have been my God"* (Ps. 22:10)! His faith was like a burning flame that shone at its brightest in the darkness of Golgotha.

> *Have you ever praised the Lord Jesus for His trust? Do you sing praise to God in response to His work at Calvary? Even in the darkest hours trust in the One Who gives songs in the night (see Job 35:10)!*

"About midnight Paul and Silas were praying and singing hymns to God." (Acts 16:25)

Notes:

....

....

....

....

....

....

....

....

....

....

....

Complete Devotion

"Then Jesus, calling out with a loud voice, said, 'Father, into your hands I commit my spirit!' And having said this he breathed his last." (Luke 23:46)

The holy body of Jesus had been abused to the utmost by the scourging and crucifixion. Isaiah writes, *"His appearance was so marred, beyond human semblance, and his form beyond that of the children of mankind"* (Isa. 52:14). Then the great waters of God's judgment entered His holy soul, so that He had to lament, *"Look and see if there is any sorrow like my sorrow, which was brought upon me, which the LORD inflicted on the day of his fierce anger"* (Lam. 1:12). Finally, after all this was over, His human spirit, which He had received from God, was to be separated from His body.

One last time He cried out in a loud voice, *"Father, into your hands I commit my spirit"*! No one else could have shouted out loudly in such agonizing pain on the cross. But although He possessed this supernatural power, He didn't use it to save Himself. Instead, He trustingly surrendered His spirit into the hands of Him Who had sent Him. This commandment He had received from His Father—and He obeyed Him unto death!

The Lord Jesus lived in dependence on God and died in dependence on God. How wonderfully the Father responded to His Son's complete surrender: After three days, He used His divine power and glory to raise Him from the dead, the One Who had glorified Him so perfectly here on earth. He gave Him all power over heaven and earth (see Mt. 28:18) and finally received Him into glory. There He now sits at the right hand of the Majesty—exalted *"far above all rule and authority and power and dominion, and above every name that is named"* (Eph. 1:21)—crowned with glory and honor (see Heb. 1:4; 2:9).

The Son of God didn't hold back anything in His life. He surrendered Himself unreservedly to God and finally even gave up His spirit into the hands of the Father. Abraham had not withheld his beloved son from God and was richly blessed in return. Paul and Barnabas had given their lives for the name of the Lord Jesus and were therefore entrusted with a special task (see Acts 15:25–26). Paul had been able to say, *"I do not account my life of any value nor as precious to myself"* (Acts 20:24). With this attitude He had more joy in prison later on than most Christians living in freedom today. Letting go and relying on the Lord is connected with great reward and blessing!

> *Are there still things you cling to and withhold from God, or does He really have one hundred percent control over your life? What does it mean practically for you to present your life to God as "a living sacrifice, holy and acceptable to God" (Rom. 12:1)?*

Notes:

....

....

....

....

....

....

....

....

....

....

....

....

....

....

....

....

Victory through Death

"Father, into your hands I commit my spirit!" (Luke 23:46)

Along with His birth, the life and death of Jesus were unique! Luke tells us His first words spoken as a Man which are recorded in the word of God, *"Did you not know that I must be about My Father's business?"* (Luke 2:49 NKJV). The same evangelist also wrote down the last words of Jesus before His death, *"Father, into your hands I commit my spirit!"* He did not rest until He had completely fulfilled what He declared as a twelve-year-old boy.

Meanwhile the Son of God had been in the hands of men for several hours. He had told His disciples beforehand that He would be delivered into the hands of sinners (see Mt. 26:45). It was the cruel hands of these wicked men that finally crucified Him (see Acts 2:36). All that was now over. Now the time had come for Him to deliver His spirit into the faithful and powerful hands of His Father. What a contrast!

The three hours of darkness lay behind Him. But the payment was still outstanding—the price was yet to be paid, *"For the wages of sin is death"* (Rom. 6:23). He had to die! There was no way around it. In order to defeat him who through the power of death, kept mankind in fear and trepidation, He Himself had to go into death (see Heb. 2:14–15). That's why He gave up His spirit.

He had already announced a wonderful result of His death to the thief on the cross: *"Today will you be with me in paradise"* (Luke 23:43). Through His death, death—which is the king of terrors for unbelievers (see Job 18:14)—has become the gateway to paradise for believers!

> *How strong is your desire to leave this world behind "and be with Christ" (Phil. 1:23)? The great Shepherd, Who has taken care of you every day until now, will also be with you if God wants you to walk, held by His hand, through the valley of the shadow of death (see Ps. 23:4)!*

"The eternal God is your dwelling place, and underneath are the everlasting arms."
(Deuteronomy 33:27)

Notes:

....
....
....
....
....
....
....

Trusting God: For Time and Eternity

"Father, into your hands I commit my spirit!" (Luke 23:46)

The Father's hand is the place of eternal security, from which nothing and no-one can ever be seized (see John 10:29). The Lord Jesus had entrusted His disciples into these mighty hands—and into these same hands He now placed His spirit. He did so like someone who hands over a treasure to be looked after by someone in whom he has complete trust. Because He trusted God so unreservedly, He could say even when faced with death, *"My flesh also dwells secure. For you will not abandon my soul to Sheol, or let your holy one see corruption."* (Ps. 16:9–10).

The following applies to each of us: *"What do you have that you did not receive?"* (1 Cor. 4:7). Instead of clinging to what we have received by grace, we may give it back and entrust it to Him Who, with His mighty hand, can make all things great and give strength (see 1 Chron. 29:12). David expressed this truth very well in prayer when he said, *"All things come from you, and of your own have we given you"* (1 Chron. 29:14).

Paul was able to say with conviction, based on his own experience of faith, *"I know whom I have believed, and I am convinced that he is able to guard until that day what has been entrusted to me"* (2 Tim. 1:12). What does he mean by this "deposit"? W Kelly writes, "By 'my deposit' is to be understood all that I as a believer entrust to the safekeeping of God, not only the security but the blessedness of the soul and the body, of the walk and the work, with every question conceivable to be raised in the past, present, or future."[11] The better you know your Savior in Whom you have believed, the more you will enjoy the grace in which you stand, and will also rest in Him with confidence in the present or future (see 2 Pet. 1:2). Isaiah encourages us with the words, *"You keep him in perfect peace whose mind is stayed on you, because he trusts in you. Trust in the LORD forever, for the LORD GOD is an everlasting rock."* (Isa. 26:3–4).

> *How well do you know your Lord? If you have entrusted the most precious thing you possess—your soul—to Him for eternity, why do you still hesitate to trust Him wholeheartedly for the short time left on this earth? The Lord is your Shepherd, you shall not be in want (see Ps. 23:1)!*

Notes:

....

....

....

....

....

11 W Kelly, *Exposition of Timothy*, Bible Truth Publishers, p. 197

The Presence of the Risen One

"Beginning with Moses and all the Prophets, he interpreted to them in all the Scriptures the things concerning himself... but they urged him strongly, saying, 'Stay with us, for it is toward evening and the day is now far spent.' So he went in to stay with them." (Luke 24:27, 29)

Three days after His crucifixion, the Son of the living God rose from the dead in the power of His incorruptible life. The Victor of Calvary is *"the living"* (Luke 24:5), *"the firstborn from the dead"* (Col. 1:18) and *"the beginning of God's creation"* (Rev. 3:14)! Never again will death reign over Him. He *"lives forever and ever"* (Rev. 15:7)!

But instead of returning to heaven immediately after His resurrection, *"the great shepherd of the sheep"* now really desired to show Himself to those for whom He had suffered such untold agony. But in this, too, He did not act prematurely or rashly. In the case of the disciples from Emmaus, He waited patiently until the Word of God was working in their hearts before He revealed Himself to them. Only after they opened their house to Him and urged Him to stay, the time had come for Him to show Himself to them.

He entered the house as a guest, but then immediately took on the role of the head of the house, who gives thanks for the food and serves it. How much He had longed for this fellowship with His disciples! It is no different today. He loves to give a deep awareness of His presence and have practical fellowship with those who love Him and keep His commandments (see John 14:21).

> *The LORD blessed the house of Obed-Edom during the time when the ark of the covenant—a picture of Christ—was in his house. What place does 'the invisible guest (host)' occupy in your home? How does this become visible in concrete terms? How do you show the Lord Jesus that you desire fellowship with Him? Keep His word and ask Him to show Himself to you anew, so that you can experience what it means when He and the Father make their home with you (see John 14:23)!*

Notes:

....

....

....

....

....

....

....

The Unchanging One

"When he was at table with them, he took the bread and blessed and broke it and gave it to them. And their eyes were opened, and they recognized him. And he vanished from their sight. They said to each other, 'Did not our hearts burn within us while he talked to us on the road, while he opened to us the Scriptures?'" (Luke 24:30–32)

After the Lord had entered the house in Emmaus, He took bread, gave thanks, broke it and gave it to the two disciples. Even on the day of His greatest triumph, He did not act recklessly, but remained the completely dependent Man, Who thanked God for the food and served the people. Just as He had thanked in former times for the five loaves and the two fish, or for the seven loaves and the few small fish, He did here also. He is the same—before and after His resurrection. This is also true with regard to His ascension, for Paul writes, *"He who descended is the one who also ascended far above all the heavens"* (Eph. 4:10).

The two disciples were downcast (see Luke 24:17). The faith of these two was only like a glowing wick which was about to go out. Isaiah had written of Christ, *"a faintly burning wick he will not quench"* (Isa. 42:3). This is exactly what we see here: He opened the scriptures to them about His Person and thereby rekindled their faith, so that a short time later they could say, *"Did not our hearts burn within us while he talked to us on the road?"* (Luke 24:32).

Are you feeling depressed and disappointed at the moment because things have turned out differently to what you had hoped? It is precisely on such days that the Lord wants to be especially close to you and give you a deep awareness of His love. God comforts those who are downhearted (see 2 Cor. 7:6)!

> We're living in the last days where, unfortunately, there is an terrible amount of failure among God's people. But it's precisely at this time that the Lord Jesus, God's faithful Witness, calls out to you personally, "Behold, I stand at the door and knock. If anyone hears my voice and opens the door, I will come in to him and eat with him, and he with me." (Rev. 3:20). Open your wounded heart to Him through a conscious decision, just as the two disciples opened their house to Him.

"Thus says the One who is high and lifted up,
who inhabits eternity, whose name is Holy:
'I dwell in the high and holy place,
and also with him who is of a contrite and lowly spirit,
to revive the spirit of the lowly,
and to revive the heart of the contrite.'"
(Isaiah 57:15)

Notes:

....
....
....
....
....
....
....
....
....
....
....
....
....
....
....
....
....
....
....
....
....
....
....
....
....
....
....
....
....

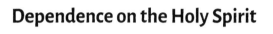

Dependence on the Holy Spirit

The Power of the Highest

"The Holy Spirit will come upon you, and the power of the Most High will overshadow you; therefore the child to be born will be called holy—the Son of God." (Luke 1:35)

Having looked at the prayer life of the Lord Jesus in some detail so far, let's now look at the place the Holy Spirit occupied in His life and what we can learn from it for our lives.

4000 years after God had announced the great Savior to mankind, He fulfilled His promise: The Seed of the woman Who was to crush the head of the serpent came into this world. Isaiah had announced the birth of the Messiah as follows: *"Behold, the virgin shall conceive and bear a son, and shall call his name Immanuel"* (Isa. 7:14).

How can it be that a virgin becomes pregnant? Mary also asked the same question. She was the chosen vessel to give birth to the Son of God, and she felt her total inability and unworthiness for this tremendous task. But God is the God Who performs miracles—and that is the case here too. It was the power of the Most High that worked to fulfill what He had announced over past centuries through His prophets, *"Nothing will be impossible with God"* (Luke 1:37)!

In sovereign grace, the Almighty had appointed Mary to this mighty task. Why? Because He wanted to glorify Himself through her. Of course, what Mary has done is unique, but we can also apply it in a broader sense to ourselves, the believers in the time of grace. Mary was to bring the Son of God into the world—we should present Him to the world through our lives (see Phil. 2:16). This is what Paul was concerned with in his ministry, because he writes, *"My little children, for whom I am again in the anguish of childbirth until Christ is formed in you!"* (Gal. 4:19). God wants Christ, as *"the fruit of the Spirit"* (Gal. 5:22–23), to be visible in believers!

He has given you everything you need to accomplish this tremendous task: The life of the Lord Jesus (eternal life) and the Holy Spirit. Paul wrote to the Galatians, *"It is no longer I who live, but Christ who lives in me"* (Gal. 2:20). The Spirit of God Who dwells in you (see Rom. 8:9–11) is the power that makes the life of Jesus visible through you (see 2 Cor. 4:10).

Robert Chapman said, "There are many who preach Christ, but not so many who live Christ. My goal will be to live Christ." He did this—and he still is a great role model for many Christians!

"Put on the Lord Jesus Christ."
(Romans 13:14)

> *Why is it important that the Son of God takes on more and more form in you and becomes visible to others? Do you trust that today—this day—the Holy Spirit will give you the strength to live Christ? Spend much time with the Lord Jesus. This is the key to allow the Holy Spirit to make you more and more like Him.*

Notes:

....
....
....
....
....
....
....
....
....
....
....
....
....
....
....
....

A Tremendous Truth

"In him all the fullness of the Godhead was pleased to dwell."
(Colossians 1:19 JND)

John the Baptist, the forerunner of the Messiah, was filled with the Holy Spirit from his mother's womb (see Luke 1:15). The Lord Jesus, on the other hand, was begotten by the Holy Spirit. He did not need to be filled with the Spirit because He was full of the Holy Spirit at all times (see Luke 4:1)! When He lay in Bethlehem's manger, His body was already the temple where the fullness of the Godhead—the Father, the Son and the Holy Spirit—dwelt in the flesh (see Col. 1:19).

Just as the grain offering was mixed with oil, so Jesus' life was also marked *perfectly* by the work of the Holy Spirit. Even from childhood, He lived under the constant guidance of the Spirit of God—not only from the moment when the Spirit came upon Him, in full sight of all at His baptism. The decisions He made as a twelve-year-old boy, and also the words He spoke at that time, proceeded from the working of the Holy Spirit in Him.

Who receives the Spirit of God today? Anyone who takes God at His word by believing in the message of the gospel of salvation (see Eph. 1:13). If you have done this, then your body is now a temple where a divine Person dwells day and night (see 1 Cor. 6:19). We owe this Person reverence, love and trust. The Holy Spirit has a specific will at all times and wants to guide you in every situation of your life. This is a tremendous truth that we forget all too quickly in everyday life.

Your body no longer belongs to you, but is a temple of the Holy Spirit and thus belongs to the One Who bought it with His blood (see 1 Cor. 6:19–20). God has separated you for Himself, has set you apart. That is why He calls you to live a holy life and to keep your body holy. He demands that you give Him your life without reservation. The Holy Spirit Who dwells in you needs a holy dwelling in order to be able to work freely in you and through you!

> *What changes would you make in your 'home' if suddenly a world-famous personality announced that he would be visiting you today? What can you do so that you are 'tidied up' on the inside? Be aware that the Holy Spirit has a will for you every day and wants to guide you in everything you think, say and do! And the Holy Spirit is more than a 'guest.' He abides in you permanently.*

Notes:

....
....
....
....
....
....
....
....
....
....
....
....
....
....
....
....
....
....
....
....
....
....
....
....
....
....
....
....
....
....

The Steamer and the Sailing Boat

"John bore witness: 'I saw the Spirit descend from heaven like a dove, and it remained on him... And I have seen and have borne witness that this is the Son of God.'" (John 1:32, 34).

It was a very special moment in the history of mankind. Jesus of Nazareth, the Son of the living God, stood in the Jordan, surrounded by sinners, to be baptized by John. As He prayed, heaven suddenly opened. God, the Holy Spirit, descended on Him in the form of a dove—and remained on Him (see John 1:32–34).

This had never happened before! In the Old Testament, the Spirit of God sometimes came upon individuals for a time to equip them for a special ministry. But after the work was done, He left them again. Even the man after God's heart prayed, *"Take not your Holy Spirit from me"* (Ps. 51:11). The Son of God, on the other hand, was the first Man on Whom the Spirit of God remained without ever leaving Him.[12]

In view of the coming of the Holy Spirit at Pentecost, the Lord Jesus said to His disciples, *"I will ask the Father,*

---

12 As mentioned earlier, the Lord Jesus possessed the Holy Spirit from birth (see Luke 1:35; Lev. 2:4). However, at His baptism, the Spirit came upon Him *visibly* to make it clear to men that He was the Christ, the Anointed of God, Who ministered under the guidance and in the power of the Holy Spirit.

*and he will give you another Helper, to be with you forever... he
dwells with you and will be in you"* (John 14:16–17). Today the
Spirit no longer comes to believers for a time, but dwells
in them permanently. This is a big difference, as the following illustration shows:

Imagine an old sailboat and a modern steamboat. The
sailboat needs an outside force to move forward. The
boat only gains speed when the wind blows. This is, es-
sentially, how it was with the believers before Pentecost,
when the Spirit came from time to time. The steamer, on
the other hand, is driven by an 'inner' force. Since the
turbine is on board the ship, the steamer is independent
of external circumstances. This corresponds to the believers after Pentecost, in whom the Holy Spirit dwells
and works uninterruptedly.

> **"You will receive power
> when the Holy Spirit has come upon you."
> (Acts 1:8)**

> *Are you just waiting for the circumstances to be favorable to move forward? Trust that the Holy Spirit Who dwells within you will give you the strength to continue despite difficult circumstances, and take steps in faith! Paul writes, "Him who is able to do far more abundantly than all that we ask or think, according to the power at work within us" (Eph. 3:20). Have you ever taken time to ponder over this verse? What things can the Spirit of God do in you that you have not yet thought possible?*

Notes:

....

....

....

....

....

....

....

....

....

....

....

....

A Divine Letter of Commendation

"On him God the Father has set his seal." (John 6:27)

From the moment the Holy Spirit came to earth at Pentecost, everyone who believes the gospel is redeemed by the blood of Jesus and sealed with the Holy Spirit (see Eph. 1:13). God imprints, figuratively speaking, His stamp on the person and says: This person belongs to Me—for time and eternity!

Imagine a farmer who wants to buy sheep. After he has paid the price for them, he marks them with his initials. Why does he do that? To show that they are his property, and so that he can recognize one if it gets lost. The payment of the price entitles them to be his possession and the mark identifies them as his own. It is similar to when God seals a believer with His Spirit: The blood of Christ is the price with which God has bought you, and the Holy Spirit is the divine seal that marks you as His property.

It was different with the Son of God: He was publicly sealed with the Spirit because of His personal perfection (see John 6:27)! For 30 years He had lived blamelessly before the eyes of God. Now He received divine recognition from heaven for His perfectly consecrated life. The Father publicly placed His seal on Him, so to speak, to make it clear that this Man was quite different from all those who were baptized by John in the Jordan. He is the only man who was sealed with the Holy Spirit before blood was shed.

If you let the Holy Spirit work freely within you, the Lord can use this as a divine letter of commendation to the people you deal with. *"It is not the one who commends himself who is approved, but the one whom the Lord commends"* (2 Cor. 10:18). When the Spirit of God works in you and through you, it will become visible. Paul writes in reference to his ministry to the Corinthians, *"You show that you are a letter from Christ delivered by us, written not with ink but with the Spirit of the living God"* (2 Cor. 3:3). Faithful and dependent servants of God are characterized by the fact that the Spirit can work freely in them (see 2 Cor. 6:3, 6)!

The following example, given by HL Heijkoop from his own experience, illustrates how the Holy Spirit can guide when we make ourselves available to Him:

"Eighteen years ago, I went to America for the first time. My wife and I were on the way to a town where there was a fellowship where we knew a few brothers. But on the way, the Lord said to me, 'You must go to such and such a town.' This was a completely different place! I had never been there, did not know a single person, and I did not have any names or addresses. I was forced to make a detour of hundreds of kilometers to get the address of a brother in that town.

Now, we arrived there on a Saturday evening and were warmly welcomed. We stayed until the following Thursday. During that time, my host told me something about the relationships in the local fellowship. As I said, we did not know the brothers and sisters, or their circumstances. As usual, every evening there was a meeting and the Lord used me to preach the Word.

Finally, on the Wednesday evening, some of the brothers came up to me to talk to me. They said that the situation in the fellowship had become so miserable and there had been such division that they had decided this week to split up. But, they said, the Lord had sent me and the proclamation of the Word had made it clear to them that a split was not good. So because of this, they were not going to split up, but remain together. So the Lord had sent me there, even though I did not know anything about all these things."[13]

> *How does your life show that you are a servant of the Lord and a letter of Christ to the people around you? How does your life differ from the life of an unbeliever, who doesn't have the Holy Spirit?*

---

13 HL Heijkoop, *The Leading of the Holy Spirit*, Believer's Bookshelf Inc., Canada, p. 14–15

Notes:

....
....
....
....
....
....
....
....
....
....
....
....
....
....
....
....
....
....
....
....
....
....
....
....
....
....
....

The Dove and the Fire—An Important Exhortation

"When Jesus was baptized, immediately he went up from the water, and behold, the heavens were opened to him, and he saw the Spirit of God descending like a dove and coming to rest on him." (Matthew 3:16)

The Holy Spirit had long been searching for a resting place on earth, just as the dove had been in the days of Noah after the great flood. After 4000 years of human history, He had finally found it in the heavenly Man (see 1 Cor. 15:47). Isaiah, looking at Christ, writes, *"the Spirit of the LORD shall rest upon him"* (Isa. 11:2).

The Servant of God was at all times *"holy, innocent, unstained, separated from sinners"* (Heb. 7:26). In Him purity, sinlessness, meekness, and humility were presented truly and bodily before the eyes of the people. This also applies to the first 30 years that He lived before the eyes of God. Not once did He grieve the Holy Spirit during this time. Everything He thought, said and did happened under His guidance and glorified God. The Lord Jesus is the only Man in Whom the Spirit constantly had the freedom to influence every movement of life!

Why did the Holy Spirit descend on the Son of God in physical form, like a dove, while He appeared to the disciples at Pentecost in the form of divided tongues as of fire (see Acts 2:3)? Because with Him there was nothing to be judged by fire. The grain offering was without leaven (see Lev 2:11) and Christ was without sin. John writes, *"in him there is no sin"* (1 John 3:5). The disciples, on the other hand, although they had already been saved, still had the sinful flesh in them, which always fights against the Spirit (see Gal. 5:17). This did not change after the Holy Spirit was poured out.

Paul admonishes the Ephesians, *"Do not grieve the Holy Spirit of God, by whom you were sealed for the day of redemption."* (Eph. 4:30). What does this mean practically for your life? Since the Spirit of God is holy, He will be grieved if you tolerate sin in your life. He sees the pictures and movies you watch, and He also hears the music you listen to. He also takes note of each thought you nourish, each word you speak, and everything you do in public or secret. That's why it's very important that you regularly review your life and practice self-judgment, as Paul writes, *"Let us cleanse ourselves from every defilement of body and spirit, bringing holiness to completion in the fear of God"* (2 Cor. 7:1).

No idle word should come out of the mouth of a Christian. Blasphemy, anger, and any evil behavior grieves the Holy Spirit and dulls His work in us (see Eph. 4:29–31). How quickly such things happen to us when we give room to the flesh! But there's another way: the Lord Jesus never talked badly about others. He never lost His temper and didn't argue with the Pharisees when they attacked and insulted Him. Instead, as Isaiah writes about Him, *"I will put my Spirit upon him... He will not quarrel or cry aloud, nor will anyone hear his voice in the streets"* (Mt. 12:18–19).

> *Are you aware that the words you speak and the things you look at can have a very concrete negative influence on the work of the Spirit in you? How often do you honestly examine your life before God and practice self-judgment?*

"Set a guard, O Lord, over my mouth;
keep watch over the door of my lips!"
(Psalm 141:3)

Notes:

....

....

....

....

....

....

....

....

....

Prayer and the Workings of the Spirit

"When Jesus... was praying... the Holy Spirit descended on him." (Luke 3:21–22)

Where there is serious prayer, heaven acknowledges it—and it often happens in connection with the working of the Holy Spirit. The Man of prayer was also the Man Who was daily in dependence on the guidance and power of the Spirit of God.

The connection between prayer and the work of the Spirit is striking in the New Testament: 120 men and women were united in prayer when the Holy Spirit came at Pentecost and gave them the ability to witness to the great things of God in different languages (see Acts 1:14; 2:11). Under threat from the Jews, the disciples prayed for boldness to speak the word of God to the people. Then they were all filled with the Holy Spirit and testified with great power to the resurrection of Jesus (see Acts 4:29, 33). Saul of Tarsus was praying when Ananias was sent to lay hands on him to fill him with the Holy Spirit (see Acts 9:11, 17). Peter also spent some time in prayer before the Holy Spirit spoke to him and told him where to go (see Acts 11:5, 12).

We're not praying today for the Holy Spirit to come upon the earth—this happened about 2000 years ago. Instead, we can ask that we be more filled with the Spirit, and that the Spirit can work more within us and within the local assembly. Paul prayed that the Ephesians would be strengthened with power by His Spirit in the inner being (see Eph. 3:16). The Apostle desired that God would give the Romans to abound in hope by the power of the Holy Spirit (see Rom. 15:13).

The Spirit teaches believers to pray and increases the longing for the coming of the Lord Jesus. This becomes especially clear on the last page of the word of God, where it says, *"The Spirit and the Bride say, 'Come'"* (Rev. 22:17)! As a general rule, if we pray with sincere hearts, we sow to the Spirit (see Gal. 6:8) and thereby give Him liberty to work in us, for the flesh has no place in the presence of God!

The following incident recounted by Georg von Viebahn shows us the influence prayer can have on the work of the Spirit: "A servant of God was in B_____ for the proclamation of the Gospel. His friend with whom he was staying said one morning, 'I would like to ask you to visit a sick believer this morning; she has been in a lot of pain for three years and would certainly be happy to see you.' She was a severely tried child of God, a factory worker who had not only been disfigured and incapacitated by an accident, but who had also been afflicted by unspeakable pain through severe internal injuries.

The evangelist visited the sick person in the morning, who greeted him with the words, 'I am very happy that you have come, but you have no idea what your visit means to me. Imagine, when I started my day this morning, I prayed, "Lord, you know that I cannot go to gospel meetings where others have so much blessing. If you think it is good, send the brother to visit me; but, Lord, only if You think it is good.'"

God had heard this childlike prayer and through His Spirit had given instruction to the evangelist's landlord so that he, unaware of what he was doing, asked his friend to visit the sick woman."[14]

The fact that there are many examples in God's Word, and beyond, where the work of the Holy Spirit is directly related to prayer should be another motivation for us to spend more time in prayer!

> *Do you give the Spirit of God time and space to redirect your thoughts when you pray? Do you pray to the end that you will be more filled with the Spirit and that the work of the Spirit in the local assembly would increase? Prove the Lord whether He does not, by His Spirit, give particular strength in service and testimony for Him, if you recommit to pray more for it!*

---

14   Georg von Viebahn, *Geleitet durch den Heiligen Geist* (from *Schwert und Schild*), 1907, Ev. Allianzblatt

Notes:

The Seven Spirits of God

"The Spirit of the LORD shall rest upon him, the Spirit of wisdom and understanding, the Spirit of counsel and might, the Spirit of knowledge and the fear of the LORD. And his delight shall be in the fear of the LORD." (Isaiah 11:2–3)

The sevenfold mention of the Holy Spirit in these verses shows us His fullness and perfection. One day, when Christ will rejoice here as *"Lord of lords and King of kings"* (Rev. 17:14), these seven attributes of the Spirit of God will be fully displayed in Him.

But even during the approximately 33 years that He spent here on earth at His first coming, this spiritual fruit became visible in His life. It was the Spirit of the LORD Who came upon Him at His baptism, for Isaiah writes, *"I have put **my** Spirit upon him"* (Isa. 42:1). How blatant, therefore, was the insult of His enemies, who insinuated that He had a demon and was casting out evil spirits through Beelzebub (see John 7:20; 8:48, 52; Mt. 12:24, 27)!

"Behold, my servant shall act wisely" (Isa. 52:13), God had said with regard to His faithful Witness. He was fully equipped for this by the Holy Spirit. On the one hand, the Lord Jesus revealed the nature of God in this world through the Spirit; on the other hand, the Spirit filled Him with power for ministry and with the knowledge and will of His Father.

The Son of God is still today the One Who has *"the seven spirits of God"* (Rev. 3:1)—the fullness of the Holy Spirit. He introduced Himself thus to the assembly in Sardis, which had an outwardly pious confession, but was in fact spiritually dead (see Rev. 3:1). Unfortunately, in many parts of Christendom today, the work of the Holy Spirit is almost extinguished by human organization and the activity of the flesh. Nevertheless, the fullness and power of the Spirit is still unreservedly at the disposal of those overcomers who live at the end of the time of grace! Also today, the Spirit of God wants to give you wisdom, understanding, advice, strength and knowledge, and lead you to true fear of God.

Before you go into the meetings, do you pray that the Lord will speak to you? Do you expect Him to give you answers to questions through prophetic ministry? The following incident, once reported by HL Heijkoop, encourages us to anticipate the guidance of the Holy Spirit more when we come together as a local assembly:

"A few years ago, a brother and his wife from the Netherlands received the conviction that the Lord wanted to send them to Colombia. The brother asked the Lord, 'What should I do? I have the gift neither of a teacher nor of an evangelist. So what should I do in Colombia?' Neither spoke to anyone about it, but in the course of the next six months, the Lord kept telling them that they should go to Colombia.

One Sunday morning, the brother was praying while he was cycling to the meeting, and said, 'Lord, if it really is Your will that I go to Colombia, please give me a word at this meeting that makes this very clear.'

That afternoon, a brother was talking about obedience. In this he said, 'If the Lord tells you that you should go to Colombia, then you should go to Colombia!' He did not know anything about the preoccupations of this brother. But now this brother knew well enough, and he thanked the Lord for that. He later said to me, 'The brother who was speaking could just as well have used Africa as an example, but he said Colombia.' Is it coincidence or the leading of the Holy Spirit when the Lord gives such an answer?"[15]

> *Why does the Lord Jesus present Himself to the assembly in Sardis as the One Who has the fullness of the Spirit of God? Don't follow the crowd, but be an overcomer who trusts in the guidance of the Holy Spirit both in his personal life and in the life of the assembly!*

---

15 HL Heijkoop, *The Leading of the Holy Spirit*, Believer's Bookshelf Inc., Canada, p. 18–19

Notes:

The Spirit of Wisdom and Understanding

"The Spirit of the LORD shall rest upon him, the Spirit of wisdom and understanding." (Isaiah 11:2)

The Gospels show us many events in which the attributes of the Holy Spirit became visible in the life of Jesus:

Even as a child, He was filled with wisdom and continued to increase in wisdom (see Luke 2:40, 52). When He went to Jerusalem with His parents at the age of twelve, He knew that the time had come for Him to remain behind in the temple. Although He had more understanding than all His teachers and had more insight than the aged (see Ps. 119:99–100), He did not teach there, but behaved appropriately for His age. It was very wise of Him to ask questions in this situation and to speak only when He was asked something. The scribes were amazed when they heard His answers, which brought to light His deep understanding of the Word of God (see Luke 2:46–47).

When the Lord was tempted by Satan in the desert, the Holy Spirit gave Him the wisdom to wield the *"sword of the Spirit"* (Eph. 6:17) in such a way that the enemy put to flight. A short time later He taught in Nazareth in the synagogue. Under the guidance of the Spirit, He spoke prophetic words that revealed the state of His opponents' hearts.

The Lord Jesus could distinguish spirits and also the motives of those who came to Him (see 1 Cor. 12:10). With much wisdom and understanding, He answered the questions as to whether it was right to pay taxes to Caesar and how that was connected with the resurrection of the dead. His answers amazed His opponents and closed their mouths at the same time (see Mt. 22:33–34).

He judged things not on what He heard or saw (see Isa. 11:3), but in the light of the Holy Spirit. Just as the seven-branched lampstand spread light in the Holy Place of the tabernacle, so the Spirit of God gave light to the Son of Man to judge all that came before Him with divine wisdom and understanding.

Are you about to have a difficult conversation? Or are you afraid because you don't know what to say when you are suddenly asked to answer for your faith? The Son of God gave the disciples a wonderful promise that you too can rely on in such situations: *"When they bring you before the synagogues and the rulers and the authorities, do not be anxious about how you should defend yourself or what you should say, for the Holy Spirit will teach you in that very hour what you ought to say... For it is not **you** who speak, but the Holy Spirit"* (Luke 12:11–12; Mark 13:11). Stephen experienced this (see Acts 7)—and you can still experience it today!

> *Trust that the Spirit will guide you in the conversations that are before you today! Do you rely on human wisdom and rhetoric when preaching the Word of God or spreading the gospel, or do you consciously depend on the guidance of the Spirit (see 1 Cor. 2:13)? Strive to prophesy under the guidance of the Spirit, or to speak the words of God (see 1 Pet. 4:11)!*

Notes:

....

....

....

....

....

....

....

....

....

....

....

....

....

....

The Spirit of Counsel and Might

"The Spirit of the LORD shall rest upon him... the Spirit of counsel and might" (Isaiah 11:2)

The Spirit of counsel enabled the Lord Jesus to make the right decisions and to instruct others in the will of God. The Spirit of might helped Him put decisions made into practice (see Isa. 9:6). There are also many examples of this in His life.

After 40 days in the wilderness the Servant of God, under the guidance of the Spirit, decided to return to Galilee to begin His public ministry. The Spirit gave Him the strength to walk this path even though He had not eaten for 40 days (see Luke 4:14).

It was certainly not an easy decision for Him to choose His twelve disciples. They were to accompany Him and be at His side for over three years. He knew how much misunderstanding they would demonstrate towards Him, that Peter would deny Him and eventually all would leave Him. Eleven of them would also have the tremendous task of judging the tribes of Israel (see Mt. 19:28). The dependent Servant spent a whole night in prayer before making this far-reaching decision (see Luke 6:12–13). Later He once said, *"Did I not choose you, the twelve? And yet one of you is a devil"* (John 6:70). Although He knew this from the beginning (see John 6:64), the Spirit gave Him the strength to make this decision—and to continually bear with it.

The Spirit of counsel was also revealed in the many teachings that the Lord passed on to His disciples (see Mt. 5–7, for example). He taught them according to their understanding (see Mark 4:33). At the same time, His teaching, which He placed before their hearts in the power of the Holy Spirit, was with authority—contrary to the way the scribes preached (see Mark 1:22).

Every day the Lord Jesus lived in dependence on the Holy Spirit. This marked Him out as the perfect Man. The enemy repeatedly tried to dissuade Him from going to Golgotha. But He, in the power of the Spirit, steadfastly set His face to do what He was commanded to do (see Luke 9:51). The decision to take the cup of suffering out of His Father's hand also required strength, which the Holy Spirit gave Him, while an angel sent by God physically strengthened Him.

Are you facing an important decision right now? The same Spirit Who led the Lord Jesus wants to help you make the right decision! The first Christians also experienced this (see Acts 15:28; 16:7). Do you sometimes make decisions with the conviction that the Holy Spirit led you in them? Trust that the Spirit of God will give you the strength to make decisions in dependence on Him!

Notes:

....

....

....

....

....

....

....

....

....

....

....

....

....

....

The Spirit of Knowledge and of the Fear of the LORD

"The Spirit of the LORD shall rest upon him... the Spirit of knowledge and the fear of the LORD. And his delight shall be in the fear of the LORD." (Isaiah 11:2–3)

The Spirit of knowledge and fear of the LORD was shown on the one hand in Jesus' understanding of His Father's thoughts, and on the other hand in His complete agreement in heart with Him. Solomon writes that the fear of the LORD is the beginning of knowledge. It also involves hating evil (see Prov 1:7; 8:13). Both are clearly seen in the life of Jesus.

He knew that His Father's house should be a house of prayer (see Isa. 56:7). But the wickedness of men had made it a den of thieves. With holy zeal He championed His Father's concerns by condemning that which was out of place in the temple. The Gospels mention this both at the beginning and the end of His public ministry (see John 2:15–17; Mt. 21:12–13). He was angry at this wickedness without ever committing sin, because *"in him there is no sin"* (1 John 3:5)—and He did not let the sun set on His anger (see Eph. 4:26)!

The fear of the Lord also manifests itself in reverence and respect. Jesus enjoyed honoring God and doing what pleased Him. As early as the age of twelve He had said to His parents, *"Did you not know that I must be about My Father's business?"* (Luke 2:49 NKJV). He served God with devotion and faithfulness, never testing Him inappropriately (see Mt. 4:5–10).

He acknowledged the LORD in all His ways and therefore also experienced how He made His paths straight (see Prov 3:6). When He was rejected by men, He accepted it from His Father's hand. Even during this time He rejoiced in the Spirit, praising the Father and justifying Him for His ways (see Luke 10:21). He knew that God had chosen the weak and the despised of the world so that He would receive the glory for everything (see 1 Cor. 1:26, 29). That is why we see Him so often together with the outcasts of society, so that His enemies even accused Him of being *"a friend of tax collectors and sinners"* (Mt. 11:19).

The Spirit of God wants to lead us into the enjoyment of the wonderful relationship we have with the Father and the Son—into the joy of eternal life (see John 4:14). He wants to show us the things that God has given us in Christ (see 1 Cor. 2:9–10). But He will only do this if we are occupied with things that please Him, for *"the one who sows to the Spirit will from the Spirit reap eternal life"* (Gal. 6:8).

> With what zeal do you stand up for the
> interests of God? How does the fear of
> God become clearly evident in your life?
> Pray that you will get to know your Lord
> better and that He will open your eyes to
> His amazing works!

*"The people who know their God
shall stand firm and take action."*
(Daniel 11:32)

Notes:

....

....

....

....

....

....

....

....

....

....

....

....

....

A Man Full of the Holy Spirit

"Jesus, full of the Holy Spirit... was led by the Spirit" (Luke 4:1)

Luke tells us that the Lord Jesus was full of the Holy Spirit when He was led into the wilderness. This is the first time that the Word of God says something like this about a person. There are some people who have been filled with the Spirit for special tasks. But the expression *"full of the Holy Spirit"* goes beyond that: it speaks of a permanent state.

The Lord was not occasionally filled with the Holy Spirit, but His whole life was continuously marked by the work and guidance of the Spirit. With Him there was no occasional switching between a 'spiritual' and a 'normal' life—as is unfortunately the case with us sometimes. His every feeling, every thought, every word and every action was influenced by the Spirit of God.

Stephen is also explicitly said to have been *"a man full of faith and of the Holy Spirit"* (Acts 6:5). When this faithful man stood before the Jewish Sanhedrin, the Holy Spirit spoke through him and gave him the strength to be a faithful witness to his Lord (see Mark 13:11; Acts 1:8). Full of the Holy Spirit, he fixed his eyes on heaven and saw the glory of God—and Jesus standing at the right hand of God (see Acts 7:55).

The Spirit of God opened Stephen's eyes to the glory and greatness of the Son of God (see John 16:14). And what was the result? As he contemplated the glory of the Lord, the Holy Spirit made the life of Jesus visible in his body in the hour of his death (see 2 Cor. 3:18; 4:10).

> *Do you also experience that the Holy Spirit makes the Son of God so great to you that you speak of Him from the fullness of your heart? Is this a pious theory for you, or a reality of faith? Do you often have a certain switching from a 'spiritual' to a 'normal' life? Purpose in your heart to give the Holy Spirit permanent freedom so that He can work in you unhindered!*

Notes:

....

....

....

....

....

....

....

....

....

....

The Confidence of Faith and the Working of the Spirit

"He was a good man, full of the Holy Spirit and of faith." (Acts 11:24)

The *"founder and perfecter of our faith"* (Heb. 12:2) was always both in prayer (see Ps. 109:4) and full of the Holy Spirit (see Luke 4:1). He lived in permanent dependence, and at the same time had uninterrupted trust in the guidance of the Spirit. The New Testament shows us some believers who, to a certain extent, imitated the example of their Master and have thus become role models for us.

Barnabas, for example, was a good man, full of the Holy Spirit and of faith. The *"Son of encouragement"* had a heart that beat with brotherly love for his brothers and sisters in faith. He was characterized by a personal willingness to sacrifice (see Acts 4:36–37) and thereby fulfilled John's exhortation, who wrote, *"Little children, let us not love in word or talk but in deed and in truth."* (1 John 3:18).

It is noticeable that in both Stephen and Barnabas the expression, *"full of the Holy Spirit,"* is associated with faith. These men had complete trust in the guidance of the Spirit and experienced in practice how He led them daily. It is one thing to know fundamentally that the Holy Spirit dwells within me, and something completely different to surrender myself unreservedly to the Spirit of God, and every day consciously give the guidance of my life over to Him. This requires trust!

At the same time, it is a learning process to recognize the voice of the Holy Spirit. Georg von Viebahn writes, "When the young Samuel had begun his ministry in the tabernacle in Shiloh, he did not yet know the voice of the Lord. He believed he heard a human voice and needed instruction to recognize God's voice (see 1 Sam. 3). Thus, many children of God are not initially able to recognize the voice of the Holy Spirit, especially when He, warning them, wants to withhold a step, decision, or word. It may not necessarily be something that is bad or untrue in itself, but God warns His child because He sees the beginning of a path that leads into disaster and difficulty...

... It's often the same with something you're about to say. The thing may be true, and the heart without hatred toward the people you want to speak about. But there is an inner voice that warns: 'Don't say that!' You hold back; but how often does it happen that a few minutes later you blurt out what was on the tip of your tongue? As soon as it is out, one person takes up this from what was said, and another takes up that; thus, the conversation takes a slanderous, sometimes even evil course. The child of God must say to himself: 'I'm to blame!' The Holy Spirit had warned the believer so that he wouldn't become unable to be a witness for the Lord Jesus in his interaction with the world."[16]

> *Is it visible in your life that faith works through love (see Gal. 5:6)? How do you experience spiritual guidance in your life? Trust that the Spirit also wants to guide you today in decisions, conversations and work!*

Notes:

....

....

....

....

....

....

....

....

....

....

....

....

....

---

16 Georg von Viebahn, *Geleitet durch den Heiligen Geist* (from *Schwert und Schild*), 1907, Ev. Allianzblatt

The Pen of a Ready Scribe

"He whom God has sent utters the words of God, for he gives the Spirit without measure." (John 3:34)

The seven things that the Lord Jesus says about the Holy Spirit in John 16:13–14 make it clear that He is a divine Person:

- He *is coming.*
- He *guides.*
- He *hears.*
- He *speaks.*
- He *glorifies.*
- He *receives.*
- He *declares.*

The Lord Jesus received the Holy Spirit as a Man without any hindrance. Here on earth He was the holy Vessel through Whom the Holy Spirit spoke as a Person without interruption—for God *"gives the Spirit without measure."* Every word He spoke was a word from God. Even the servants sent by His enemies to catch Him out testified, *"No one ever spoke like this man!"* (John 7:46). The sons of Korah wrote prophetically about Him, *"You are the most handsome of the sons of men; grace is poured upon your lips"* (Ps. 45:2).

We, too, have received the Spirit as a divine Person without restriction. Under His guidance, we are also able at any time to say what God wants to communicate in that moment. Peter writes, *"Whoever speaks, as one who speaks oracles of God"* (1 Pet. 4:11). However, this will only happen if we really live in dependence on the Holy Spirit.

How serious it can be if we do not listen to the voice of the Holy Spirit, is made clear by the following true story recounted by Georg von Viebahn:

"A young believer was drafted into military service as a sergeant. One afternoon, whilst in charge of the firing squad, he arrived at the shooting range half an hour too early, and therefore entered a pub garden to drink a cup of coffee before starting his shift.

He hadn't been sitting there long, when a lieutenant from the same battalion came, ordered coffee and sat down at the same table. The sergeant had a powerful urge to tell the young officer a word of the saving grace found in Christ. He said in his heart: 'Tell him; witness the gospel to him!' But his mind reasoned against it: 'We only have a little while; what will he think; he is your superior!' etc. Soon the time had passed—they got up and began target practice.

After the shift the sergeant went home. When he entered the barracks next morning, the first thing he heard was, 'Did you know that Lieutenant X shot himself last night?' It was the officer to whom the disciple of Jesus should have spoken the message of grace once again. It had been the voice of the Holy Spirit Who wanted to entrust this message to the otherwise-so-faithful one who confessed his Lord."[17]

> *How often do you think of the fact, that the Holy Spirit wants to use you to speak His words every day and that your tongue is an instrument of God that He wants to use? The Psalmist says, "My tongue is like the pen of a ready scribe" (Ps. 45:1)! Make this your prayer for today!*

*"Walk in wisdom toward outsiders,
making the best use of the time."
(Colossians 4:5)*

Notes:

....

....

....

....

....

17 Georg von Viebahn, *Geleitet durch den Heiligen Geist* (from *Schwert und Schild*), 1907, Ev. Allianzblatt

Filled with the Holy Spirit

"Do not get drunk with wine, for that is debauchery, but be filled with the Spirit." (Ephesians 5:18)

With the Lord Jesus there was nothing that could have hindered the working of the Spirit in any way. He lived a life that was completely focused on God, and He pursued the same goals as the Spirit of God. In all areas of life He was under the Spirit's constant influence and allowed Himself to be led by Him.

The Word of God gives us many examples of people who have been filled with the Holy Spirit in order to be enabled to do a special work for God. This shows us how important the ministry of the Spirit is to the Lord! Nevertheless, it may well be that there are believers who perhaps have never been filled with the Spirit, because they have never given Him the liberty or place in their hearts.

How do you recognize that a person is filled with the Holy Spirit? How does such a person behave? If the Spirit of God is the only Source of your thinking, then you are filled with Him. A person filled with the Spirit is also someone through whom the mind and life of Jesus can be seen.

A drunk person is characterized by the fact that alcohol influences his behavior, and he does things he would not otherwise do if he were sober. A man filled with the Spirit shows the fruit of the Spirit (see Gal. 5:22–23) and does things that he would not do without the Spirit.

This brings us to the question of how someone can be filled with the Holy Spirit. What do we have to do? First of all, we should be aware that the Holy Spirit doesn't fill us from the outside, but from within—because He dwells in believers. When a visitor comes to your home, you have to decide how many rooms you want to give him access to, and which rooms you want to be kept only for your private use. It is the same with the different areas of your heart that the Spirit wants to fill.

Moreover, a vessel can only be completely filled with something if it has been emptied of everything else beforehand. If you want to be filled with the Spirit, you must be ready to separate yourself from all that grieves the Spirit, Who then takes His place in your heart. When the cloud of the LORD's presence filled the temple, the priests had to leave. The Holy Spirit, too, cannot fully display His presence in the hearts of children of God until they give Him the liberty to do so. The Spirit of God cannot share the throne of your heart with your self-will!

It makes a big difference whether a person wants to use divine power to get what he wants, or whether he gives himself completely to his Lord so that He can use him as He wants! The example of the first Christians makes it clear that being filled with the Holy Spirit is also connected with our prayer life: *"When they had prayed, the place in which they were gathered together was shaken, and they were all filled with the Holy Spirit and continued to speak the word of God with boldness"* (Acts 4:31).

> *Does the Holy Spirit belong to you or do you belong to the Holy Spirit? Remove anything that could grieve the Spirit from your life, and give Him the freedom to fill your whole heart!*

Notes:

....

....

....

....

....

....

....

....

....

....

....

....

....

Overcome Evil with Good

"Do not be overcome by evil, but overcome evil with good."
(Romans 12:21)

For 40 days the Son of God was led about in the wilderness by the Holy Spirit. During this time, He always used the sword of the Spirit to ward off Satan's vile attacks. In this way, He repeatedly overcame evil with good. His struggle was not against blood and flesh, but against the cosmic powers over this present darkness (see Eph. 6:12). He fought with the armor of God and in faith resisted the adversary until he finally left Him for a time (see Luke 4:13).

The Word of God invites us not only to separate ourselves from evil, but also to engage in good things that promote the working of the Spirit. For example, we should not only stop lying, but speak the truth. It is not just a question of no longer stealing from others, but rather of sharing with anyone in need. Idle words no longer have any place in our mouths. Uplifting words that are for the benefit of others should mark us now. Moreover, instead of bitterness, wrath, anger, clamor and slander, kindness, tenderheartedness and forgiveness should now be seen in us (see Eph. 4:25–32).

Trying to avoid evil without doing good at the same time automatically leads to a pathological, legal life of faith. Biblical separation is always away from evil and toward

God—and toward the good works He has prepared for us beforehand in which we should walk (see Eph. 2:10).

The separation from bad things prevents the Spirit from being grieved. The practice of good things promotes His working in us! In this context it is interesting to note that the filling of the water jars in John 2 happened before the purification of the temple. The negative things in our lives will disappear to the extent that we consciously pursue the good!

> *Are you striving today to take advantage of the opportunities God gives you to "do good to everyone, and especially to those who are of the household of faith" (Gal. 6:10)? God has prepared good works for you. Do you have your eyes opened to see these things? Look for opportunities today in which you can overcome evil with good—in the power of the Spirit!*

Notes:

....

....

....

....

....

Sow to the Spirit

"The one who sows to his own flesh will from the flesh reap corruption, but the one who sows to the Spirit will from the Spirit reap eternal life." (Galatians 6:8)

The Son of God came to give us eternal life, i.e. *"have life and have it abundantly"* (John 10:10). The Holy Spirit, Whom the Father sent in the name of the Son (see John 14:26), leads us into the enjoyment of this life (see John 4:14). The more we sow to the Spirit, the more we will actually embrace (i.e. enjoy) the eternal life to which we have been called (see 1 Tim. 6:12). The harvest also involves seeing the fruit of the Spirit in us and in this God is glorified.

What are the positive things that we can do or with which we can be *"filled"* to promote the work of the Spirit in us? The following eight examples can help us to display more fruit of the Spirit and enjoy eternal life with delight today:

- In the Epistle to the Colossians Paul writes, *"Let the word of Christ dwell in you richly"* (Col. 3:16). The "rich" study of the Word of God is a key to a life filled with the Spirit of God.
- The Apostle gives us another key in Philippians 4:8: *"Finally, brothers, whatever is true, whatever is honorable, whatever is just, whatever is pure, whatever is lovely, whatever is commendable, if there is any excellence,*

if there is anything worthy of praise, think about these things." Reflecting on these positive things promotes the action of the Holy Spirit.

- Prayer is also a key that opens the door to the Holy Spirit. Through Him we have access to the Father (see Eph. 2:18), and at the throne of grace—in the presence of God—the Spirit fills us with confidence and boldness.

- Whilst we contemplate the life and glory of the Son of God, the Spirit is also doing a work in us: He is transforming us more and more into the image of our Lord (see 2 Cor. 3:18).

- The Holy Spirit has the goal of glorifying Christ. This happens, for example, when we sing spiritual songs to the glory of God. In this way we make ourselves one, so to speak, with the intention of the Spirit, so that He can work freely in us (see Eph. 5:18–19).

- The first Christians devoted themselves to the fellowship of the apostles and lived practically in self-sacrificial brotherly love (see Acts 2:42; 4:32–33). Practical fellowship in the family of God—with those who possess the same eternal life—strengthens our spiritual life. The Spirit Himself wants to maintain this practical fellowship; and if we strive for it ourselves, then we are at one with Him (see Phil. 2:1; 2 Cor. 13:14).

- The Spirit of God dwells both in the individual believer (see 1 Cor. 6:19) and in the house of God (see 1 Cor. 3:16). It is the Spirit's intention to work in the place where Christians gather to the name of Jesus. Therefore, attending the meetings of the local assembly where we come into the presence of the Lord Jesus is also something we sow to the Spirit.

- Last but not least, the Holy Spirit rejoices when we occupy ourselves with heavenly things and have a heavenly mind. Paul writes, *"Seek the things that are above, where Christ is, seated at the right hand of God. Set your minds on things that are above"* (Col. 3:1–2). The Spirit will occupy us with heavenly things if we direct our thoughts towards them (see 1 Cor. 2:9–10)!

> *Do you long to be filled with the Holy Spirit? Be occupied with the positive things that promote the work of the Spirit! When was the last time you sacrificed anything material to advance the Kingdom of God?*

"If then you have not been faithful in the unrighteous wealth, who will entrust to you the true riches?"
(Luke 16:11)

Notes:

The Son and the Sons of God

"Jesus was led up by the Spirit into the wilderness to be tempted by the devil." (Matthew 4:1)

Mark reports that the Holy Spirit drove the Lord Jesus into the wilderness straight after His baptism and that He immediately obeyed the directing of the Spirit (see Mark 1:12). He served in the power of the Spirit—from that moment until the end of His life of service. Luke tells us that He was full of the Holy Spirit, and that the Spirit not only led Him to the place of temptation, but also guided Him whilst He was there for those 40 days (see Luke 4:1).

Dependence also means allowing yourself to be led by someone. This is exactly the attitude that the Servant of God adopted at the very beginning of His public ministry. The Holy Spirit was His Guide, just as the pillar of cloud had been for the people of Israel in the wilderness (see Num. 9:17–23).

Paul writes in the Epistle to the Romans, *"All who are led by the Spirit of God are sons of God."* (Rom. 8:14). So it is the distinguishing feature of the sons of God that they are led by the Holy Spirit! God calls this their 'normal condition.' The guidance of the Spirit in this context is connected with self-judgment and overcoming evil. Through the Spirit, God has given us the strength we need not to give in to temptation, but to be overcomers every day (see Rom. 8:2, 13).

Georg von Viebahn writes the following in his article, *Geleitet durch den Heiligen Geist (Guided by the Holy Spirit)*: "Just as the Holy Spirit warns in some cases, He also drives in other cases. The leading of the Holy Spirit, the driving to divinely ordained steps, encompasses many different areas. He reminds believers of the poor who need support, of sick people who need to be to be visited, even of small domestic duties which we are about to overlook. For example, as many accounts demonstrate, He uses a believer to send exactly the right amount of money on a specific day for a work of God, so that this amount arrives at precisely the right time to where there was earnest pleading for this particular need!"[18]

---

18 Georg von Viebahn, *Geleitet durch den Heiligen Geist* (from *Schwert und Schild*), 1907, Ev. Allianzblatt

> *Do you consider that you are normally led by the Spirit of God when you live in sincere fellowship with God? What are the hindrances to instantly obeying when the Spirit makes it clear to you that you should do something? Trust that the Spirit of God will make you an overcomer to sin today if you let Him work and exercise the necessary self-judgment!*

Notes:

....

....

....

....

....

....

....

....

....

....

....

....

....

....

....

In the School of God

"Jesus, full of the Holy Spirit, returned from the Jordan and was led by the Spirit in the wilderness for forty days, being tempted by the devil." (Luke 4:1–2)

How did the Son of God know that right now was the proper moment to go into the wilderness? The baptism in the Jordan had been, so to speak, the starting point for His public ministry. Hadn't the Father just publicly approved Him before the people? Wouldn't it have been the obvious thing to immediately start preaching the gospel of the kingdom in public with this 'tailwind'? But instead of following human logic, the Lord Jesus followed the guidance of the Spirit—and He led Him first of all into the wilderness, where He was to suffer temptations under the hand of Satan.

Jacob was alone with God when he received the name 'Wrestler of God' (Gen. 32:28). Joseph spent more than two years in prison before publicly becoming a blessing to many. God used Moses to lead the people of Israel out of Egypt after having prepared him for 40 years in the land of Midian. David first had to be hunted like a partridge on the mountains before he assumed public authority over Israel. Elijah spent a long time at the brook Cherith and then with a poor widow before he took up his task alone on Carmel with 850 evil prophets. Shortly after his conversion Paul was sent by the Lord to Arabia for about two years; and

John was banished to the island of Patmos when he wrote about the future of the world. These men were all trained by God in seclusion and prepared for immense tasks.

God's lessons are very different from what the world teaches us. Moses had been taught all the wisdom of the Egyptians and Paul had learned at the feet of Gamaliel. But in the school of God—in many dark hours—these men learned what they needed to know to become faithful servants of God. The Son of God told His disciples, *"What I tell you in the dark, say in the light, and what you hear whispered, proclaim on the housetops"* (Mt. 10:27).

Temptations and trials should do to us what a storm does to an oak tree—they make us become more deeply rooted in the love of God and the Son of God (see Eph. 3:17; Col. 2:7). Just as the color on porcelain only acquires lasting strength through the action of heat, so we often learn patience and perseverance for our life of faith only through suffering, in which we experience our God and get to know Him ever better (see Rom. 5:3).

> *"Let steadfastness have its full effect,*
> *that you may be perfect and complete, lacking in nothing."*
> *(James 1:4)*

> *Do you always only do things that are logical, or do you also give the Spirit the freedom to guide you 'in extraordinary ways'? To what extent do you let God shape and prepare you? Have you long been rowing against the wind? Don't give up!*

Notes:

....

....

....

....

....

....

....

....

....

....

....

....

....

....

....

....

....

Obedience and the Leading of the Spirit

"Jesus, full of the Holy Spirit, returned from the Jordan and was led by the Spirit in the wilderness for forty days, being tempted by the devil." (Luke 4:1–2)

The Spirit's guidance is closely associated with obedience. But what does obedience actually mean? Obedience means doing the will of another. That is why the Son of God came into this world and said, *"I have come down from heaven, not to do my own will but the will of him who sent me"* (John 6:38).

After the Lord Jesus proved His obedience at His baptism in the Jordan, the Spirit immediately led Him into the wilderness. Under the temptations of Satan, He demonstrated obedience as it had never been seen before in 4000 years of human history. There, for 40 days, He was obedient under the most difficult circumstances, while the Spirit 'led Him about'!

A few years later, the Lord sent out two of His disciples to find the place where He wanted to eat the Passover with them. He asked them to follow the man with the water jug—a picture of the Holy Spirit giving us direction through the Word of God. He asked them to depend on this man and trust his guidance. Just because they 'let go' and obeyed the word of the Lord, they experienced how

He led them to the place where they could have fellowship with their Master (see Mark 14:12–16).

In the Old Testament, it took more than 400 years for the man after God's own heart (see 1 Sam. 13:14)—through deep spiritual exercise—to find the place where God wanted to dwell and be worshiped (see 1 Chron. 21). God hasn't given us an address of a building where we should gather with Christians in the name of Jesus. But we can find this spiritual place under the guidance of the Spirit, if we leave our own ideas aside and are ready to obey the Word of God unconditionally.

God gives the Holy Spirit to those who obey Him (see Acts 5:32). The Spirit in turn guides those who are obedient when the Lord gives them a task. Philip also experienced this when he obeyed the voice of the angel, even though his commission was more than unusual. The evangelist, having cast out the gospel net in Samaria and made a great catch, was now to go under the guidance of the Spirit to a barren place to fish for a special 'fish.' He had no idea what a blessing his obedience would mean for Africa—because it is certain that the Ethiopian treasurer brought the gospel to this continent (see Acts 8)!

"I say, walk by the Spirit."
(Galatians 5:16)

> *Are you ready to be a blessing to Africa if God calls you? Have you ever put aside your personal preferences and sincerely asked the Lord, 'Where do you want us to meet together?' (see Mt. 26:17). The question that was already asked of Rebekah with regard to Abraham's servant arises anew for each of us today: "Will you go with this man?" (Gen. 24:58). This means that you consciously entrust the Spirit of God with the guidance of your life—even if He may lead you in ways you never thought possible. Are you ready for this?*

Notes:

....

....

....

....

....

....

....

....

....

....

....

....

The Power of the Stronger One

"If it is by the Spirit of God that I cast out demons, then the kingdom of God has come upon you." (Matthew 12:28)

The Son of God came into this world to destroy the works of the devil (see 1 John 3:8). But how was this to happen in practice? First of all, He had to bind Satan, *"the strong man"* (Mt. 12:29), to free people from the power of darkness. Until that moment *"that ancient serpent"* (Rev. 12:9) had been the victor over men. Often it was the case that when he tried to deceive a person, they failed and thereby succumbed to him, the *"ruler of this world"* (John 12:31; 16:11).

In the wilderness, the adversary tried to dissuade the Son of God from serving God in dependence. But he had no success with Him. With regard to Christ, Satan's hands were tied from the beginning. Suddenly the strong man faced a stronger One, to Whom he was inferior. Now Satan had to watch helplessly as the Son of God penetrated his sphere of power and snatched away his spoils (see Mt. 12:29).

The words *"I... by the Spirit of God"* are characteristic of the whole life of Jesus. He was full of the Holy Spirit, led by the Spirit, and overcame the power of the enemy in the strength that the Spirit gave Him. Everything He did was done by the Spirit of God. He never acted independently of Him.

It's interesting to note that the first miracle of the Lord Jesus in Luke's Gospel is that He cast out a demon (see Luke 4:35). In whose strength did He do this? He could easily have cast out evil spirits in His own divine power. But that is exactly what He did not do! Instead, He tells the Pharisees, *"But if it is by the Spirit of God that I cast out demons, then the kingdom of God has come upon you"* (Mt. 12:28).

How often this happened! Let us think of the Gadarene who was possessed by an entire legion of demons, or the boy who was thrown into the fire by a particular type of demon. Even the seven demons who had taken possession of Mary Magdalene had to give way to the power of the Spirit.

His enemies accused the Son of God of casting out demons by Beelzebub, the *"prince of the demons"* (Mt. 9:34). What a grievous insult! By attributing the perfect work of the Spirit in Jesus' life to satanic power, they blasphemed against the Holy Spirit—and were therefore lost forever (see Mark 3:22, 28–30).

Can a believer lose the Holy Spirit if he sins? It is true that we can grieve the Spirit of God. But it is very interesting that God assures us on this very point, where we are warned against it, that we have been sealed with the Spirit for the day of our redemption (see Eph. 4:30)—and accordingly He remains in us all our lives. This divine seal, which identifies us as God's property, cannot be 'sinned away.'

The Lord Jesus Himself assured His disciples that the Holy Spirit would be with them for all eternity (see John 14:16). You too are God's possession for time and eternity!

The incident in the wilderness is an impressive demonstration that the One Who is in us, is greater than the one who is in the world (see 1 John 4:4). Demons are still active in our day. Today we are especially dealing with their teachings which they spread in Christianity (see 1 Tim. 4:1). The world rulers of this darkness often disguise themselves as 'angels of light' and use, for example, supposed 'tongues' and 'miracle healings' to imitate the work of the Holy Spirit and thereby seduce believers (see 2 Cor. 11:13–15).

> *Remind yourself anew that the power of the Spirit can still break the chains of people who are in bondage today! Why does God assure us that the Holy Spirit is greater than the spirit who rules this world? Ask God to give you "according to the riches of his glory he may grant you to be strengthened with power through his Spirit in your inner being, so that Christ may dwell in your hearts through faith" (Eph. 3:16–17)!*

Notes:

Serving in the Power of the Spirit

"Jesus returned in the power of the Spirit to Galilee." (Luke 4:14)

For 40 days the Son of God fasted in the wilderness. Luke, the faithful doctor, expressly writes that He was hungry at the end of those days (see Luke 4:2). How weak He must have felt after almost six weeks without food! But right now the time had come for Him to return to Galilee to begin His public ministry.

The question is how was He to walk so far in this physical state. He walked—but not in His own power. He used the power of another that was at His disposal. It was the Spirit of God Who helped Him in His exhaustion and enabled Him to begin His ministry.

Why does Luke mention these details here? Surely, it was also to show us that the Lord Jesus undertook all His ministry in the power that God gave Him. His voluntary renunciation of natural energy, which He otherwise received through food, made this all the more apparent. He made Himself dependent both on the guidance and the power of the Spirit. The Psalmist writes, *"His delight is not in the strength of the horse, nor his pleasure in the legs of a man, but the LORD takes pleasure in those who fear him, in those who hope in his steadfast love."* (Ps. 147:10–11). What joy God had in His Servant, Who waited patiently, trusting in His goodness at all times, and relying absolutely on His power!

To Zerubbabel the Lord said these encouraging words: *"Not by might, nor by power, but by my Spirit"* (Zech. 4:6). Paul also had this experience. After he had been stoned by the Jews and declared dead, he got up again, went back to the city and continued his ministry the next day (see Acts 14:19–22). Was it not the Spirit of God Who gave him the strength? To the same Apostle the glorified Lord said, *"My grace is sufficient for you, for my power is made perfect in weakness"* (2 Cor. 12:9).

We, too, are called not to serve in our own power, but in the power that God gives—so that He may be glorified in everything (see 1 Pet. 4:11)! Our extremities are God's opportunities—this is especially true when we are weak and exhausted. If the Spirit of God is our Guide, He will show us when it is time to serve and when it is time to rest. There are situations in life where one is tired and yet continues (see Jud. 8:4).

The following true event illustrates how crucial it sometimes can be to overcome fatigue and obey the voice of the Holy Spirit:

"In the small town of L___, a believing Christian, N___, had gone to bed at about 9 o'clock in the evening, after the day's work was finished. Suddenly the thought came to him: you should to go to X___ now! X___ was a believer who had become unfaithful, who had brought much dishonor to the Lord through his evil way of life. He had separated himself from the children of God, who rebuked him earnestly; he now went his way alone.

X___ lived far away on the other side of the city. N___ therefore rejected the strange thought that had risen in him, especially as he was tired. But that thought intensified in him like a warning, like an order: 'Go to X___!' In the end he could not resist the conviction that it was an instruction from God to go there. He got up, dressed and left.

Arriving in front of X___'s house, he only saw illuminated windows on the second floor; he knocked on the locked front door and noticed someone coming down. The door was unlocked from the inside and X___ stood in front of him, asking him, 'What brings you here, what do you want?' 'An inexplicable urge drove me here; I didn't know what I should do, but I had to come to you!' 'This is really miraculous,' X___ replied. 'When you knocked on the front door, I was standing on a stool with a noose around my neck, pulling the rope through the lamp hook on the ceiling to hang myself! When there was a knocking downstairs I thought, You could just go and see who is knocking so late in the evening.'"[19]

19   Georg von Viebahn, *Geleitet durch den Heiligen Geist* (from *Schwert und Schild*), 1907, Ev. Allianzblatt

God had proved here by facts the truth of what is written: *"As I live, declares the Lord GOD, I have no pleasure in the death of the wicked, but that the wicked turn from his way and live; turn back, turn back from your evil ways, for why will you die, O house of Israel?"* (Ezek. 33:11).

A blind man can see the intervention of God here. He can speak in such a way that His voice cannot be misunderstood! Was it not the Holy Spirit Who led this man and drove him by force to do the will of God in grace, to protect the despairing man?

> *Whose power do you rely on when you serve God? When you are tired and exhausted, remember: "He gives power to the faint, and to him who has no might he increases strength" (Isa. 40:29). Does your attitude towards your weaknesses imitate that of Paul, who could say, "For the sake of Christ, then, I am content with weaknesses, insults, hardships, persecutions, and calamities. For when I am weak, then I am strong" (2 Cor. 12:10)? Be obedient when the Spirit gives you an assignment!*

Notes:

S

Streams of Living Water

"He that believes on me, as the scripture has said, out of his belly shall flow rivers of living water. But this he said concerning the Spirit, which they that believed on him were about to receive; for the Spirit was not yet, because Jesus had not yet been glorified." (John 7:38–39 JND)

The power in which the Lord Jesus returned from the desert was now to unfold in His public ministry. If the people of God are said to be *"like a watered garden, like a spring of water, whose waters do not fail"* (Isa. 58:11), how much more does this apply to the true Servant of God? The fruit of the Spirit was seen in Him as in no other!

Streams of living water were now to emerge out of the body that had just fasted—for the blessing of large crowds and all those who came to Him in faith. Peter remembers this time years later when he said, *"Jesus... went about doing good and healing all who were oppressed by the devil"* (Acts 10:38). All this happened through the work of the Spirit in Him!

The belly of man is the place that is never permanently satisfied, but always in need of food. Paul writes that there are people whose god is their belly, i.e. who give natural needs and personal satisfaction the highest place in life (see Phil. 3:19).

For Christians, on the other hand, it's from this very place—through the Spirit of God—that a permanent abundance should flow forth, as the Lord's words in John 7:38 show. Christ not only wants to satisfy our personal needs, but He also wants to make us channels of blessing for others through the Holy Spirit. We're not only anointed with the Spirit, but our cup should also overflow (see Ps. 23:5). This is done, among other things, by experiencing the joy of hope through the power of the Spirit and passing it on to others (see Rom. 15:13).

By the way, it is characteristic of the Holy Spirit that He flows uninterruptedly. We see this, for example, in the story of Elisha with the widow, when the oil—an image of the Holy Spirit—flowed as long as there were empty vessels to receive it (see 2 Ki. 4). The emptier we are of ourselves, the more the Spirit can fill us!

> *What does the following verse mean to you personally: "All my springs are in you" (Ps. 87:7)? God wants to make you a channel of blessing for other people! What can you do to be a special help to others today? (See Acts 18:27.)*

Notes:

Anointed Kings and Royal Priests

"He came to Nazareth, where he had been brought up. And as was his custom, he went to the synagogue on the Sabbath day, and he stood up to read. And the scroll of the prophet Isaiah was given to him. He unrolled the scroll and found the place where it was written, 'The Spirit of the Lord is upon me, because he has anointed me to proclaim good news to the poor.'" (Luke 4:16–18)

The first anointing that is communicated to us in God's word happened when Jacob poured oil onto a stone in Bethel and erected it as a monument to the house of God (see Gen. 28:18; 31:13). From that moment on this stone was consecrated to God—and therefore was distinguished from all other stones. This is also the meaning of the anointing that the Lord Jesus experienced in the Jordan. The Lord's chosen Servant was publicly separated from men to serve God (see Isa. 42:1–2).

In the Old Testament kings, priests and prophets were anointed for their public service. Therefore, David called Saul *"the LORD's anointed"* (1 Sam. 24:6). With David himself, the anointing to become king happened years before he began his reign over Israel. From the day the oil touched his head, his thoughts were directed toward his calling—and this of course influenced his behavior.

The history of the people of Israel clearly shows that all kings, priests or prophets have failed in one way or another. But Christ—the Anointed One of God—never failed! Above Him heaven opened both at the beginning and at the end of His public ministry—and each time nothing but praise and approval could be heard.

God anointed us, the believers of the time of grace, with the Holy Spirit and made us *"a kingdom, priests"* (Rev. 1:6). As holy priests, our ministry consists of entering into the sanctuary—the presence of God—to worship Him there (see 1 Pet. 2:5). As royal priests, we come out of the presence of God to tell people how wonderful God is and to display His Son in our lives (see 1 Pet. 2:9). Both worship as well as the testimony to the world happen *"by the Spirit of God"* (Phil. 3:3; see Acts 1:8).

By the way, king's sons sit at the king's table. They don't dig in the garbage or cover themselves with dirt. If we want to live worthy of our calling, we must, among other things, put into practice the royal law, which says, *"You shall love your neighbor as yourself"* (James 2:8). The *"King of kings"* (Rev. 17:14) came to this earth and set an example for us—continually, for years, day after day.

True love is the opposite of egotism and manifests itself through sacrifice and devotion. It is focused on the good of others. Disciples of Jesus are to be recognized by their love towards one another (see John 13:35). Love is also the first quality mentioned in the fruit of the Spirit (see Gal. 5:22)!

> *As a holy priest, do you give praise to God daily for what He is in Himself, and for what He has done and is doing, or do you limit this to Sundays? How does your love for God manifest itself, and that you love your neighbor as yourself? When was the last time you brought the Lord Jesus to the people around you and "proclaimed good news to the poor"?*

Notes:

....

....

....

....

....

....

....

....

....

....

....

....

....

The Anointing of the Holy One

"Your holy servant Jesus, whom you anointed." (Acts 4:27)

The faithful witness of God made clear right at the beginning of His public appearance what His ministry consisted of and Who had given Him the authority to exercise this ministry. In the synagogue in Nazareth, He read from the book of Isaiah the words, *"The Spirit of the Lord is upon me, because he has anointed me to proclaim good news to the poor. He has sent me to proclaim liberty to the captives and recovering of sight to the blind, to set at liberty those who are oppressed, to proclaim the year of the Lord's favor"* (Luke 4:18; see Isa. 61:1–2). Years later Peter looks back and testifies, *"God anointed Jesus of Nazareth with the Holy Spirit and with power. He went about doing good and healing all who were oppressed by the devil, for God was with him."* (Acts 10:38). God not only sealed His Son with the Spirit because of His personal excellence (see John 6:27), but also publicly authorized Him for His ministry by anointing Him with the Spirit!

John wrote to the children of God, *"You have an anointing from the Holy One, and you know all things"* (1 John 2:20 NKJV). By the anointing with the Holy Spirit we are fundamentally able to understand the thoughts of God (see 1 John 2:27). The Spirit of God, Who wants to lead us into the whole truth, gives even young believers the ability to distinguish the voice of the Good Shepherd from the voice of a stranger (see John 10:4–5).

However, in practice we will only have this spiritual discernment if we also live spiritually. Paul writes, *"The spiritual person judges all things"* (1 Cor. 2:15). The Corinthians, on the other hand, were carnal because they had envy and strife among themselves. Therefore, they could not make progress in understanding the truth (see 1 Cor. 3:2–3).

In His grace, God has given teachers to His church who have written valuable explanations of the Word of God. It would be presumptuous to say that we no longer need these 'aids' today. At the same time, however, there is a great danger that such Bible commentaries will distract us from thinking about the Scriptures for ourselves— thereby losing great blessings and spiritual growth! Bible teacher John Nelson Darby writes, "Nothing is more harmful than this laziness which prefers to dwell on a few thoughts[20] rather than fathom the divine Word itself, which latter is denied to the soul who does not earnestly seek of the Lord, with diligence, spirituality and devotion, the knowledge which He alone can give."[21] CH Spurgeon summed it up as follows: "Read many good books, but live in the Bible."

---

20 The author refers to the thoughts of Bible expositors.
21 JN Darby, Preface *Synopsis*, Vol. 1

> *Do you prayerfully reflect on the Word of God? Paul writes to Timothy, "Think over what I say, for the Lord will give you understanding in everything" (2 Tim. 2:7). Do you trust that God will show you His will when you have the simple desire to do His will alone? If this is the case, then you will also know from which source the doctrine comes (see John 7:17)!*

Notes:

....

....

....

....

....

....

....

....

....

....

....

....

....

....

....

Wanted: Prophets!

"Earnestly desire... that you may prophesy." (1 Corinthians 14:1)

Whether the Son of God preached to the crowds or spoke to individuals, everything happened under the guidance of the Holy Spirit. In the synagogue in Nazareth, He prophesied by bringing the right message for the moment to the hearts of the listeners. Those present were amazed at the words of grace that came out of His mouth (see Luke 4:18–22).

But His prophecies consisted not only in encouraging words, but often also in exhortation. After the state of the listeners' hearts had been revealed in the synagogue, He said, *"But in truth, I tell you, there were many widows in Israel in the days of Elijah, when the heavens were shut up three years and six months, and a great famine came over all the land, and Elijah was sent to none of them but only to Zarephath, in the land of Sidon, to a woman who was a widow."* (Luke 4:25–26). Through these prophetic words He placed the Jews in the light of God, whereupon, furious with rage, they expelled Him out of the city to cast Him down a mountain.

Jesus' words were spirit and life—always in grace, but seasoned with salt. Therefore He was not afraid to preach the truth under the guidance of the Spirit and to lay it on the consciences of the listeners. He was free from the fear of man. Because He trusted in God, He was protected by Him (see Luke 4:29–30; Prov 29:25).

How is it with us today? The guidance of the Spirit and prophecy are things that can happen every day and are not limited to particular occasions of ministry or times. Those who do not learn to be led by the Spirit in everyday life will hardly be able to count on being led suddenly, 'at the push of a button', in local church meetings or public ministries.

Paul writes, *"Do not quench the Spirit. Do not despise prophecies, but test everything; hold fast what is good."* (1 Thess. 5:19–21). We quench the ministry of the Spirit in meetings if, for example, we do not take time wait for the Lord and the guidance of the Spirit, and instead give place to self-will! How great is the danger of someone getting up hastily out of fear that someone else might beat him to it? Or how quickly it happens that someone preaches only because he can no longer bear the silence of five or ten minutes!

JN Darby spoke very fittingly about the ministry of prophecy, "Yesterday ignorance was the predominant sin, and so teachers were needed. Today we often have to deal with the bluntness of conscience—for this the voice of a prophet is necessary. ... To grasp a truth and to be grasped by the truth are two very different things! Shouldn't we cry out to God for true prophets, men of godly ways who are gifted to speak earnestly, forcefully and without regard to our own reputation? ... No one says that love forbids the practice of such a gift. Love calls for it."[22]

> *Do you pray that prophecy will occur? Are you willing to be despised and rejected by brothers and sisters in the faith if you have the impression that the Spirit is leading you to name wrong-doing openly in accordance with God's thoughts? "So, my brothers, earnestly desire to prophesy" (1 Cor. 14:39)!*

Notes:

....

....

....

....

....

....

....

....

....

....

22 Translated from the German. *Ermunterung & Ermahnung*, 1957, CSV-Verlag, p. 136

The Fruit of the Spirit

*"Joseph is a fruitful bough, a fruitful bough by a spring"
(Genesis 49:22)*

The Lord Jesus was like a tree planted by brooks of water
(see Ps. 1:3). He bore fruit for God continually by *always*
doing the Father's will and revealing Him before the eyes
of the people. If we want to know how the fruit of the
Spirit (see Gal. 5:22–23) manifests itself in a person's life,
we must study His life. Here are a few thought-provok-
ing pointers.

The Son of God proved His love for His Father through
His obedience, which culminated in Him giving His life.
He had loved His disciples—to the uttermost (see John
13:1). He rejoiced in the Spirit and was joyful even in
the most appalling circumstances in which He praised
the Father for His ways (see Luke 10:21). In the midst of
danger, hatred and animosity, He enjoyed an unshakable inner peace that transcended all understanding (see
Mark 4:37–38; John 18:1–11). With what long-suffering
He endured His undiscerning disciples—for more than
three years—in the spirit of love! He took His time to
calmly dismiss the crowd and spoke, even to those who
disparaged Him, with remarkable kindness. He walked
tirelessly, doing good and showing people the goodness
of God (see Acts 10:38). He was *"the faithful and true witness of God"* (Rev. 3:14) in this world, Who let nothing and

no-one dissuade Him from serving His God faithfully. When He was attacked and slandered, He didn't defend Himself, but showed a meekness that far exceeded that of Moses. His self-control was also unique: He fasted in the wilderness for 40 days, got up regularly before dawn, spent whole nights in prayer, and always waited patiently for God's timing.

To His disciples the Master once said, *"I chose you and appointed you that you should go and bear fruit and that your fruit should abide"* (John 15:16). What exactly does He mean by these words? How can we bear fruit for God now, in our everyday life? The context of John 15 makes it clear that this fruit is the life of the Vine being revealed in the branches. We bear fruit for God when the life of the Lord Jesus—Who lives in us in the power of the Spirit—is seen in us. This is precisely the *"fruit of the Spirit"* (Gal. 5:22).

When we strive to love, to rejoice, to be at peace, to be patient with others, to show kindness, to do good, to serve faithfully, to respond gently, and to purposefully walk the path of a disciple, then we are in harmony with what the Spirit of God wants to produce in us. He will bring these things forth in us if we are willing and if we give Him the liberty to do so!

> *What is the highest goal in your life? Does your will conform to the mind of the Holy Spirit? Strive to this end that the fruit of the Spirit may be seen in you daily!*

Notes:

....
....
....
....
....
....
....
....
....
....
....
....
....
....
....
....
....
....
....
....

The Power of the Eternal Spirit

"Christ, who by the eternal Spirit offered himself without blemish to God." (Hebrews 9:14)

For 33 years the Lord Jesus did the will of His Father and lived a consecrated life of devotion. The Spirit gave Him the power to fast in the wilderness for 40 days, to resist the temptations of Satan, to cast out demons, and to heal people from their diseases. Especially in the Gospel of Luke, in which the humanity of the Lord Jesus is in the foreground, we read that *"the power of the Lord was with him,"* He healed in this power and performed miracles (see Luke 5:17; 6:19; 8:46).

But the greatest sacrifice of His life was still before Him: He was to be crucified in weakness (see 2 Cor. 13:4). When the Servant of God finally hung there on the accursed tree between heaven and earth, the word from Psalm 22:15 was fulfilled: *"My strength is dried up like a potsherd."* But it was precisely in this place of extreme weakness that He accomplished the greatest work of His life! In what power did He do this? He sacrificed Himself to God in the power of the eternal Spirit! He was the only One Who could accomplish this unique work—and He did it!

Are you faced with a great task and don't know where to find the strength to accomplish it? Do you feel weak and incapable of facing challenges that stand before you like a mountain? Do not forget that the eternal Spirit of God, Who dwells in you, always wants to give you the necessary strength to do God's will.

God wants to work in you first, before He works through you! He wants to strengthen you by His Spirit in your inner being; that Christ may dwell in your hearts, being rooted in His love (see Eph. 3:16–17). But not only that: in the power of the Holy Spirit, He can even do things in you that you would never have thought possible, as Paul writes, *"who is able to do far more abundantly than all that we ask or think, according to the power at work within us"* (Eph. 3:20).

> *Do you sometimes wonder when you look back over time, about how God has changed you, or people around you? No matter what task God gives you, He will give you the power through the Spirit to accomplish it. He can do much more in you and through you than you think! What should the consciousness of the indwelling of the eternal Spirit of God produce in you?*

Notes:

....

....

....

The Triumph of the Crucified One

"I have dealt with all that Jesus began to do and teach, until the day when he was taken up, after he had given commands through the Holy Spirit to the apostles whom he had chosen." *(Acts 1:1–2)*

Crucified, dead and buried. It's incredible to think that these things happened to the *"Lord of glory"* (1 Cor. 2:8) and the *"Author of life"* (Acts 3:15)! But His story doesn't end in the tomb. After He deeply humbled Himself, God exalted Him in a unique and wonderful way! He was made alive by the Spirit, raised from the dead by the glory of the Father, received into heaven and finally crowned with glory and honor at the right hand of the Majesty in the highest place! He now sits there, exalted *"far above all rule and authority and power and dominion, and above every name that is named"* (Eph. 1:21). He lives for God—and by God's power (see Rom. 6:10; 2 Cor. 13:4).

From His baptism to His resurrection, He was *"justified in the Spirit"* (1 Tim. 3:16 NKJV). The Spirit affixed His seal on everything the Lord Jesus did during His life. This culminated in the Holy Spirit also being involved in His resurrection, for He is *"declared to be the Son of God in power according to the Spirit of holiness by his resurrection from the dead"* (Rom. 1:4).

Christ, the Anointed One of God, hasn't lost the Holy Spirit through His death and resurrection. The fullness of the Godhead dwelt in Him here on earth (see Col. 1:19)—and this will also be the case in heaven for all eternity (see Col. 2:9)! Luke writes at the beginning of the Acts of the Apostles that the risen Victor of Calvary gave instructions to the Apostles through the Holy Spirit! (See Acts 1:2.)

The Son of God has promised us that the Holy Spirit will be with us for eternity, regardless of whether we enter into glory through the rapture or death and resurrection (see John 14:16).

We have also received the Spirit as a pledge (deposit). It is the guarantee that we will reach glory and truly take possession of our heavenly inheritance reserved for us in the heavens (see Eph. 1:14; 1 Pet. 1:4). Moreover, the Spirit dwelling in us gives us a taste of what awaits us in heaven. The following short story gives a weak illustration of this wonderful truth:

A father wants to visit a faraway country by ship and promises to take his boy with him on his journey. He gives him binoculars for the journey. The binoculars are the son's guarantee that his father will really take him on the journey. But not only that. During the boat trip the boy takes his binoculars in his hand and looks towards the longed-for destination. Even while the other passengers on the ship still can't see anything, he already sees the mainland. The binoculars give him a clearer idea of the place they are traveling to even during the voyage. This is exactly what the Holy Spirit does: He enables us today to see with the eyes of our hearts heavenly things that God has prepared for those who love Him (see 1 Cor. 2:9).

> *When was the last time you consciously thanked God for the gift of the Holy Spirit? What are you especially looking forward to when you think about heaven? We can already say "Abba, Father" through the Spirit of sonship and enjoy this relationship; but how unfathomably great it will be when sin will no longer surround us and we will rejoice unreservedly in the "freedom of the glory of the children of God" (Rom. 8:21)!*

Notes:

....

....

....

....

....

....

Dependence on the Word of God

The Word of God in Your Heart

"Blessed is the man... [whose] delight is in the law of the LORD, and on his law he meditates day and night." (Psalm 1:1–2)

The Word of God is given to the believer in several respects: as light for the way, as food for the soul, and as a weapon in battle. This was also the case in the life of Jesus. He lived not only in a permanent attitude of prayer and under the guidance of the Spirit, but also in dependence on the living Word of God. The Word filled His thoughts and gave Him guidance—every day!

Even as a child the Son of God showed a unique interest in the Holy Scriptures. The scribes were amazed when they heard the questions of this 12-year-old boy in the temple. They were even more amazed at the answers they received from Him to their questions (see Luke 2:46–47).

When the Lord Jesus began His public ministry at the age of about 30, He knew the Word of God so well that He could quote it by heart on many occasions. Because the law of God dwelt in His heart, He was able to apply it correctly at the right time, for example, when He was tempted by the devil, the scribes, the elders, the Sadducees, or the Pharisees.

When the Bible expositor August van Ryn feared going blind, he memorized the entire New Testament and parts of the Old Testament. Many rabbis today can still recite the entire Old Testament by heart. It's amazing what the human brain is capable of!

> *What value does the Word of God have for you? To what extent are you fulfilling Paul's invitation: "Let the word of the Christ dwell in you richly" (Col. 3:16)? Take time regularly to memorize verses, chapters, letters or other books of the Bible!*

Notes:

....
....
....
....
....
....
....
....
....
....
....
....
....

Joy in the Word of God

"I rejoice at your word like one who finds great spoil." (Psalm 119:162)

The Lord Jesus had great joy in the Word of God. For Him it was not just compulsory daily reading, but a strengthening food for His human soul. He could say with the Psalmist, *"Oh how I love your law! It is my meditation all the day."* (Ps. 119:97).

Christ was born under law; and He came to fulfill the law (see Gal. 4:4; Mt. 5:17). Just as the ark of the covenant contained the two stone tablets of the Mosaic law, so the law of God was in the heart of Jesus. That's why it was His heartfelt desire and a joy to fulfill God's commandments and to do His will continuously (see Ps. 40:8). As it is written: *"I find my delight in your commandments, which I love"* (Ps. 119:47).

Jeremiah could say, *"Your words were found, and I ate them, and your words became to me a joy and the delight of my heart"* (Jer. 15:16). The prophet had internalized the words of God and rejoiced in them from his heart. With this he indicated a truth which is of fundamental importance for our spiritual life: Just as the body needs natural food, so also the *"inward man"* (2 Cor. 4:16 NKJV) must be supplied with spiritual food every day!

Today we often take it for granted that we hold the Word of God in our hands. But for many centuries this was not the case for most believers. Only with the Reformation and the invention of the art of printing did the Bible become accessible to the 'common' people. It's an invaluable privilege and an infinite blessing that we can have the Bible in our mother tongue and in a good translation in our hands today!

> *How precious is the Word of God to you, and how do you use the privilege of being able to read it daily? When was the last time you were really moved while you were reading the Bible? If you have lost the joy of reading the Bible, what can you do about it?*

Notes:

....

....

....

....

....

....

....

....

....

Daily Manna, or Spiritual Famine?

"It is the bread that the LORD has given you to eat... Gather of it, each one of you, as much as he can eat." (Exodus 16:15–16)

God told the Israelites to gather manna daily to be able to survive in the desert. For us today, this means that we should occupy ourselves every day with the Lord Jesus— the Bread of Life—as a human being here on earth. How can we do this? For example, by taking a closer look at His life in the four Gospels, and meditating on it.

When we eat something, it becomes a part of us. It is exactly the same when you engage with the Word of God— it becomes, so to speak, a part of you. Your spiritual state depends largely on how intensively you—as a "doer of the Word" (see James 1:22–23)—study the Holy Scriptures and the life of Jesus!

Someone who is malnourished lacks strength and energy. This also applies to the spiritual realm. If you neglect the occupation with God's Word, you become spiritually weak. Your fellowship with the Lord will suffer and you will lack the necessary spiritual energy to work for God.

It can even happen that you do not even notice that you are suffering from spiritual famine. Laodicea says, *"I am rich, I have prospered, and I need nothing."* The Lord, on the other hand, looks deeper and answers, you don't realize *"that you are wretched, pitiable, poor, blind, and naked"* (Rev. 3:17). So we can think we are living for God, when we are actually starving spiritually.

> *Are you occupied with the life of Jesus every day and do you take your time to meditate on it? "Whoever gives thought to the word will discover good" (Prov. 16:20). What is your spiritual strength and energy like at the moment? What can you do to avoid falling prey to the judgment of Laodicea?*

Notes:

....
....
....
....
....
....
....
....
....
....
....
....
....

The Sword of the Spirit

"It is written." (Matthew 4:4)

The Son of God used the living Word as a defensive weapon against the enemy's attacks. In the wilderness and in other places we see how He, as a dependent Man, wielded the sword of the Spirit.

To every attack of Satan, the Lord answered decisively, *"It is written"* (Mt. 4:4, 7, 10). He did so until the *"ancient serpent"* (Rev. 12:9) finally fled from Him (Mt. 4:11)—for he is powerless against the Word of God.

How often the Lord Jesus had thought about this Word in His youth! When He finally began His public ministry, He was able to quote Scripture from memory at the right moment and apply it in faith to the situation. He trusted in the power of the Word in the battle against the enemy!

The Son of God also repeatedly introduced mankind to the Holy Scriptures by saying, *"What then is this that is written," "It is written"* or *"Is it not written in your Law?"* (Luke 20:17; 19:46; John 10:34).

What can we learn from this? On the one hand, it's very helpful to learn Bible verses by heart, because you have them ready at any time. On the other hand, it is important that we trust firmly in the statements of the Word.

We can only resist the devil if we submit to the will of God and hold out the sword of the Spirit to the enemy in faith (see Jas. 4:7).

In this context, EC Hadley aptly said, "Christ did not summon a host of angels to drive the devil away or display His own eternal power as Son of God, but He did what we all need to do as dependent man. He used the Word of God. To Him it was final and sufficient. He had voluntarily taken the place on earth as a Man, so does not use any other resource but what has been given to man, namely His Word and authority. He uses the Word of God and when the weakest child of God uses God's Word with steadfast confidence in its veracity and in a spirit of submission to its authority, he hurls against the enemy a thunderbolt of omnipotent power and authority that he cannot resist but must flee. You are handling omnipotent and divine authority against the enemy when you use God's Word against him." [23]

Christ was the one to Whom the word of the Psalmist applied, *"With regard to the works of man, by the word of your lips I have avoided the ways of the violent."* (Ps. 17:4). What is it like with us? Can young Christians still lead a holy life pleasing to God in today's world, in a time when the temptations of sin surround us on all sides, for example through the internet? The timeless Word of God gives

---

23   *Grace & Truth Magazine, 1979, p. 118–119*

us the answer, *"How can a young man keep his way pure? By guarding it according to your word"* (Ps. 119:9).

> *How do you react when the devil tempts you to sin? Why is it important to trust that the Word of God does indeed give you the power to break rocks in pieces (see Jer. 23:29) and make the enemy flee? Memorize Bible verses or passages that can help you overcome the sins that often occur in your life and bring your thoughts back onto a good track!*

*"I have stored up your word in my heart,
that I might not sin against you."*
(Psalm 119:11)

Notes:

....

....

....

....

....

....

....

....

Prove the Will of God

"It is written, 'Man shall not live by bread alone, but by every word that comes from the mouth of God.'" (Matthew 4:4)

In contrast to Adam and Eve, *"the second man... from heaven"* (1 Cor. 15:47) was characterized by the fact that He consistently refused to leave the path of dependence, even when He was urged to do so by Satan in the most difficult circumstances.

Although He had the power to turn water into wine and provide for 5000 men with five loaves of bread and two fish, He did not use this power to satisfy His own human needs. Instead, He remained dependent and waited until the Father gave Him guidance. His answer to the devil marked His whole life, *"Man shall not live by bread alone, but by every word that comes from the mouth of God"* (Mt. 4:4). These are very profound words, and are worth taking time to reflect on!

The Son of God as a dependent man was not driven by His natural needs—His stomach—but by the will and the Word of God. He says here, so to speak, 'I desire to eat only when God tells Me to eat. I'd rather suffer hunger than do something that God hasn't commanded Me to do'. So He made Himself completely dependent on what the Father told Him.

A few days later He said, *"**My** food is to do the will of him who sent me and to accomplish his work"* (John 4:34). Instead of satisfying His natural hunger, He found His satisfaction in doing the will of God and being in harmony with Him. Someone put it in a nutshell, like this: "His thinking, His words, His actions and His well-being were dependent on the will of His Father. From this He drew His energy, in this He rested."

It's precisely in this that we are to become more like Him and be different from the world! Paul writes, *"Do not be conformed to this world, but be transformed by the renewal of your mind, that by testing you may discern what is the will of God, what is good and acceptable and perfect"* (Rom. 12:2). Our minds are renewed and formed daily by reading the Word of God. With this renewed mind we're able to verify and discern the will of God.

In the history of the Church, fasting has been a routine practice for some men of God. George Whitefield, for example, wrote about one of these events in his diary: "We remained in fasting and prayer until three o'clock and then departed with the firm conviction that God would do great things among us." Some time later he said, "I have sought the Lord with fasting and prayer, and He gives me the assurance that He will be with me. Who should I fear?"[24] The Indian evangelist Bakht Singh had the habit

24 Benedikt Peters, *George Whitefield, Der Erwecker Englands und Amerikas*, CLV, Bielefeld, p. 86, 223

of praying and fasting for hours every Wednesday at the seaside—and thus he experienced wonderful benefits!

> *Could it be that God also wants you to fast from time to time and consciously abstain from food for a while to be more intensely in prayer before Him? Convictions of faith often mature best when you forget yourself in the presence of God. How do you practically implement the following verse in your life: "So, whether you eat or drink, or whatever you do, do all to the glory of God" (1 Cor. 10:31)?*

Notes:

....

....

....

....

....

....

....

....

....

....

....

....

What Do You Live on?

"It is written, 'Man shall not live by bread alone, but by every word that comes from the mouth of God.'" (Matthew 4:4)

It's striking that the Lord Jesus didn't simply speak of the 'Word of God' in the desert in a general sense. He was waiting for a direct commission or a specific word that was spoken 'by the mouth of God.' In Isaiah 50:4 we see that every morning He opened His ear and allowed Himself to be instructed. In the silence of the early morning He heard the voice of God and received guidance for the day.

At the same time, the Holy Scripture was light for His way and shaped His life. The Word was the source and motive for everything He did. Without the Word He did nothing.

Trust and true dependence are shown, among other things, by not taking things into your own hands, but by waiting for God to reveal His will to us or for the peace of Christ to preside in our hearts (see Col. 3:15)

This can also mean waiting before making a decision until the Lord speaks to us specifically through His Word— even if the pressure of the circumstances may still be growing. Saul lost his kingship because he didn't withstand the increasing pressure and acted in a headstrong way, when he should have waited (1 Sam. 13:8–14). If God speaks to us through the written Word or through words of prophecy, then we can firmly rely on it in faith—that is, take Him at His word—and place our hope in it.

This will then be reflected in our prayer life, as described in Psalm 119:147, 49: *"I rise before dawn and cry for help; I hope in your words... Remember your word to your servant, in which you have made me hope."* When we live in such dependence and by faith, it can also be an encouraging testimony for others. The Psalmist was convinced of this and said, *"Those who fear you shall see me and rejoice, because I have hoped in your word"* (Ps. 119:74).

The Lord encouraged His disciples by telling them, *"If you abide in me, and my words abide in you, ask whatever you wish, and it will be done for you"* (John 15:7). Occupation with the words spoken by the Son of God also causes God to form in us prayer requests that correspond to His will and which He will therefore also answer.

> *Do you wait long enough for the Lord to speak to you, or to give you the certainty that the right time has come? When was the last time you made a decision because the Lord spoke to you specifically through His living Word or through a prophetic word? Let the living Word of God be a lamp to your feet and a light to your path in your life! (See Ps. 119:105.)*

Notes:

....

....

....

....

....

....

....

....

....

....

....

....

....

....

Dependence and Suffering

"Jesus answered him, 'It is written, "You shall worship the Lord your God, and him only shall you serve."'" (Luke 4:8)

The devil did his utmost to tempt the Lord Jesus to take a shortcut on the way to His rule over this world. Instead of following the path God had given Him through suffering to glory, the ancient serpent proposed to Him to receive dominion immediately from his hand. Satan placed only one condition on Him: that the Son of God should worship him. But instead of discussing with the devil, the Lord simply held out the written Word of God to him again. With this He said, so to speak, 'I will accept the rule of this world solely and exclusively from the hand of God. I depend on Him, I wait for Him, and I trust in Him, whatever the cost.'

The faithful Witness did not allow anything in His life to come between Him and God. In Psalm 16:4 He said, *"The sorrows of those who run after another god shall multiply; their drink offerings of blood I will not pour out or take their names on my lips."*

When the Son of God later opened His heart to His disciples and told them that He would have to suffer, be rejected and killed, the devil tried again to dissuade Him from this path—this time, however, indirectly through Simon Peter. But even there the Lord answered Him with firmness and said, *"Get behind me, Satan! For you are not setting your mind on the things of God, but on the things of man"* (Mark 8:33).

After the enemy found no point of contact with the *"Holy One of God"* (John 6:69) in Gethsemane either, he finally made a last attempt at Calvary, to prevent Him from taking upon Himself the atoning sufferings that awaited Him in the three hours of darkness. As the Lord Jesus hung there on the cross, the chief priests, scribes and elders cried out, *"He is the King of Israel; let him come down now from the cross, and we will believe in him"* (Mt. 27:42). What terrible torments would have been spared Him if He had indeed used His power at that moment and descended from the cross! But that's exactly what He had come to do: to save His people from their sins *"and give His life a ransom for many"* (Mark 10:45).

If we live a consistent life in following the Lord Jesus, we too will suffer and experience practically what persecution means (see 2 Tim. 3:12). We shouldn't always think of physical violence, for the Word shows us that slander or ridicule, for example, can also be a form of persecution (Gal. 4:29; Gen. 21:9). The devil will also do everything he can to stop us from suffering for the sake of righteousness. Peter writes in a similar context: *"Since therefore Christ suffered in the flesh, arm yourselves with the same way of thinking, for whoever has suffered in the flesh has ceased from sin, so as to live for the rest of the time in the flesh no lon-*

ger for human passions but for the will of God" (1 Pet. 4:1–2). If the devil doesn't succeed in dissuading us from the path of dependence, he has no power over us!

The Lord Jesus didn't bow the knee before the devil. But Satan will have to bow his knee one day before the eternal Son of God (see Phil. 2:10–11). God assures us in His Word that if we now persevere and suffer, we will also be glorified with Him (Rom. 8:17) and reign with Him (2 Tim. 2:12). We also have a firm promise that the God of peace will one day trample under our feet (Rom. 16:20) the *"accuser of our brothers"* (Rev. 12:10).

> *Do you also experience that Satan keeps trying to lead you away from the path of discipleship? Remember John's warning, "Little children, keep yourselves from idols" (1 John 5:21)! Remain faithful to your Lord—even if it means suffering! "But even if you should suffer for righteousness' sake, you will be blessed" (1 Pet. 3:14). How does your life show that you consider "the reproach of Christ" greater riches than "the treasures of Egypt" (Heb. 11:26)?*

Notes:

Trusting God, or Testing God?

"It is said, 'You shall not put the Lord your God to the test.'"
(Luke 4:12)

This is perhaps the most subtle and dangerous of all temptations: when the devil tempts us to gain recognition before men—and what's more, when He even uses the Word of God to do so!

Let's suppose that the Lord Jesus had actually thrown Himself down from the pinnacle of the temple and had been caught by the angels of God. This would certainly have made a tremendous impression on the onlookers and given Him much recognition. Humanly speaking, this would have been the perfect prelude to His public ministry. But He had not received a word 'through God's mouth' (see Mt. 4:4) and therefore He didn't do it. Moreover, He knew the Scriptures so well to know that Satan had incompletely quoted this passage and misapplied the Word of God.

The Lord Jesus had full confidence in the faithfulness of God. He was convinced that God keeps what He promises and would therefore keep Him in all His ways. Precisely because He trusted completely, He did not first have to put Him to the test critically or frivolously. We should never do that either!

It's quite another thing to trust God's promises and test Him in the sense that He can glorify Himself in the sight of men. In Malachi 3:10, God even challenges His people to test Him in this positive way, saying, *"Bring the full tithe into the storehouse, that there may be food in my house. And thereby put me to the test, says the L*ORD* of hosts, if I will not open the windows of heaven for you and pour down for you a blessing until there is no more need."*

This was also the concern of George Müller, who took the *"father of the fatherless"* (Ps. 68:5) at His word and relied in faith on His promises. He longed to offer God, through his life, a platform on which He could show that He had not changed and was still faithful to what He promised in His Word—and how wonderfully God actually demonstrated His faithful care through the life of this man!

We, too, may cling in faith to God's promises and pray like the Psalmist, *"Confirm to your servant your promise... Remember your word to your servant, in which you have made me hope"* (Ps. 119:38, 49).

"I the L*ORD* do not change."
(Malachi 3:6)

> *What is the difference between testing God and trusting God? To what extent do you give the Lord the opportunity in your life to show people that He has not changed, and still stands firm in His promises today?*

Notes:

....

....

....

....

....

....

....

....

....

....

....

....

....

....

....

....

....

....

Milk or Wholegrain Bread?

"The scroll of the prophet Isaiah was given to him. He unrolled the scroll and found the place where it was written." (Luke 4:17)

At the beginning of His public ministry, the Lord Jesus preached the gospel of the kingdom and taught in the synagogues of Galilee. One Sabbath day, He stood up in the synagogue in Nazareth to read the Word of God. He unrolled the long scroll and found the exact spot that was on His heart. He knew the Scriptures so well that He knew where to find what was appropriate for the moment.

The Servant of God read a passage from the prophet Isaiah and ended with the words, *"to proclaim the year of the Lord's favor"* (Luke 4:19). Actually, the sentence in Isaiah 61:2 continues as follows: *"and the day of vengeance of our God."* But the Lord deliberately left out this part. Why? Because He knew that the time for this had not yet come.

What can we learn from this? For one thing, it is very helpful for us if we know the Word of God well and know exactly where something is written. On the other hand, it is fundamentally important that we learn to apply the Word of truth correctly (see 2 Tim. 2:15) and to understand the context well, i.e. to have *"the pattern of the sound words"* (2 Tim. 1:13). This means, among other things, that we learn to distinguish the different dispensations (times and variety of ways God acts with us humans at different times through history) that God shows us in His Word. For example, if we don't distinguish between law and grace, or between God's earthly people and God's heavenly people, we'll quickly come to wrong conclusions and applications, which in turn have a concrete effect on our life of faith and lead us astray.

Today we live in the time of grace—and that is precisely why it would be completely inappropriate for us to demand revenge and retaliation for the evil that is done to us. With Israel it was different and will be different again later on, as Isaiah 61:2 makes clear.

God wants us to grow in the understanding of His Word and at some point to move from milk to solid food—and this is connected with intensive Bible study, among other things. We should not only seek uplifting thoughts, but also strive to better understand God's plans and delve into His thoughts more deeply. If we do this, we can talk about these things in prayer with God—and in this way have deeper fellowship with Him. It also trains our minds and teaches us to use the Word correctly (see Heb. 5:12–14). Paul writes, *"All Scripture is breathed out by God and profitable for teaching, for reproof, for correction, and for training in righteousness, that the man of God may be complete, equipped for every good work."* (2 Tim. 3:16–17).

> *Do you know your Bible so well that you know, for example, what the respective main themes of the letters in the New Testament are? Are you willing to invest time and energy to better understand the thoughts and plans of God? The Psalmist prayed, "Direct my steps by Your word" (Ps. 119:133 NKJV).*
> *Make that your prayer too!*

Notes:

....

....

....

....

....

....

....

....

....

....

....

....

....

....

....

Do You Read with Your Head or Your Heart?

"Beginning with Moses and all the Prophets, he interpreted to them in all the Scriptures the things concerning himself."
(Luke 24:27)

This verse encourages us to read the Old Testament and to seek Christ in it. Furthermore, Paul writes, *"Whatever was written in former days was written for our instruction, that through endurance and through the encouragement of the Scriptures we might have hope"* (Rom. 15:4). Not everything is written so that we can relate it directly to ourselves; but God wants us to be encouraged and gain trust by reading the Old Testament.

The Lord Jesus often spoke with His disciples about things that were written concerning Himself in the Old Testament (see Mt. 26:24,31; Luke 22:37). He also repeatedly explained to them that He would suffer, die and rise again. He came to fulfill the Scriptures and did exactly what the prophets had prophesied about Him.

But when the fulfillment came, the disciples did not believe. Therefore, the Lord had to rebuke them and say to them, *"O foolish ones, and slow of heart to believe all that the prophets have spoken!"* (Luke 24:25).

When the Scribes and Pharisees asked Him for a sign, He explained to them the sign of Jonah, who *"was three days and three nights in the belly of the great fish"* (Mt. 12:40). Nevertheless, we later read that His disciples did not yet know the Scriptures in regard to His resurrection (see John 20:9). It may be that we have heard or read a truth many times before—and still do not really believe it!

It's not only a matter of reading or hearing the Word of God, but most importantly how, i.e. with what attitude of heart, we do it. The Lord Jesus said to His disciples both to *"Pay attention to what you hear"* (Mark 4:24) and *"Take care then how you hear"* (Luke 8:18). The Lord once asked a teacher of the law the question: *"How do you read it?"* (Luke 10:26). The *"how"* determines whether the Word of God will bear fruit in our lives—and also whether there will be thirty, sixty, or one hundred times the fruit!

> *Do you let the Word of God judge the thoughts of your heart (see Heb. 4:12) or do you judge the Word of God? When was the last time that reading the Word brought about a definite change in your life? Isaiah writes, "But this is the one to whom I will look: he who is humble and contrite in spirit and trembles at my word" (Isa. 66:2).*
> *Does this also apply to you?*

Notes:

....

....

....

....

....

....

....

....

....

....

....

....

....

....

....

....

....

....

....

....

....

....

....

....

....

....

....

....

....

....

Dependence and Trust

Further examples of dependency

lived out in the life of Jesus

The Best Wine

"The hope of the righteous brings joy." (Proverbs 10:28)

In all the signs and miracles that the Lord Jesus did, from the changing of water into wine at the wedding in Cana (see John 2:2–11) to the disciples' catch of fish at the lake of Tiberias (see John 21)—everything always happened at exactly the right time, in dependence on God.

When the Lord was at the wedding in Cana with His disciples, the hosts were suddenly faced with a problem: there was no more wine. Against the cultural background of the time, this must have been a very embarrassing situation. When Mary heard about it, she immediately went to her son and said, *"They have no wine"* (John 2:3). Apparently, with these words, she indirectly challenged Him to use His power to deal with the problem immediately.

For many years Jesus had been subject to His parents. This phase of life was now coming to an end. Now the time of His public ministry had come. Although Mary was His mother, He didn't immediately comply with her wish, but patiently waited for God's timing. That's why He told her, *"My hour has not yet come"* (John 2:4). Just as He had waited 30 years until God's time for His public appearance, He was now waiting for the right time to perform the first sign and reveal His glory before the eyes of men!

This event makes it clear that the Lord Jesus placed the will of God above any human relationship—even that with His own mother! He later challenged His disciples to do the same when He said, *"If anyone comes to me and does not hate his own father and mother... he cannot be my disciple"* (Luke 14:26). In this respect, we can apply the word of the Apostle, *"We must obey God rather than men"* (Acts 5:29) to our lives too!

Disciples of Jesus should be vessels that willingly receive the Word of God, and vessels in which the words of their Lord abide continually—without being forgotten again. If this is the case with us and we remain in Him, the true Vine, then we will also experience more answers to prayer (see John 15:7). God will turn the patient waiting of the righteous into joy (see Proverbs 10:28), just as He turned water into wine in Cana. The "best wine" is still available today for those who are waiting for His time. Isaiah writes, *"From of old no one has heard or perceived by the ear, no eye has seen a God besides you, who acts for those who wait for him"* (Isa. 64:4).

"The disciples were filled with joy and with the Holy Spirit."
(Acts 13:52)

> *Do you wait until God makes it clear to you to do some service for Him, or are you rather guided by necessities? The Lord Jesus placed spiritual relationships above family ties (see Mt. 12:50). Do you do the same? Trust that God will bless if you wait for Him!*

Notes:

....

....

....

....

....

....

....

....

....

....

....

....

....

....

....

....

....

The Path of Blessing

"His heart was courageous in the ways of the LORD."
(2 Chronicles 17:6)

When the Son of God went about from one place to another, He also did this in dependence on His Father. He didn't make His travel plans lightly, but with prayer. He was guided by the Spirit as well as by His Father, and didn't choose the most pleasant way to reach the goal simply for pragmatic reasons.

That is why John 4:4 says, *"He had to pass through Samaria."* Since the Jews were at enmity with the Samaritans, they avoided passing through their territory when traveling from Judea to Galilee. The Lord Jesus, on the other hand, deliberately didn't take the path of least resistance, but made Himself dependent on the will of God—and that led Him right through Samaria.

In this way He experienced how the Father drew souls to Him, and led people from death to eternal life (see John 6:44 and 4:7, 41). The conversion of the woman at Jacob's well brought about a revival in this city. Certainly this experience was a special refreshment for the soul of the Son of God, which strengthened Him in ministry. The way of dependence and obedience is always also the way of blessing.

> *Do you make your travel and holiday plans with prayer and in fellowship with the Lord? Consciously look for opportunities to share the gospel when you are on the road!*

Notes:

....

....

....

....

....

....

....

....

....

....

....

....

....

....

....

....

....

God's Time

"For everything there is a season." (Ecclesiastes 3:1)

The Lord Jesus didn't live here on earth in easy family circumstances. He was the eldest of at least seven children (see Mt. 13:55–56). We often read that His relatives didn't understand Him (e.g. Mark 6:3). In one instance, it is explicitly stated that they said of Him that He was *"out of his mind"* (Mark 3:21). His own brothers didn't believe in Him and questioned His ministry. On one occasion they urged Him to show Himself publicly at the Feast of Tabernacles, saying, *"Leave here and go to Judea, that your disciples also may see the works you are doing. For no one works in secret if he seeks to be known openly. If you do these things, show yourself to the world"* (John 7:3–4).

How did He respond to this provocation which came from within His own family? He didn't allow Himself to be troubled by it. Instead, He waited patiently for guidance from His Father and told His brothers, *"My time has not yet come"* (John 7:6). The Psalmist writes, *"My times are in your hand"* (Ps. 31:15). It was exactly this trust that was evident in the life of Jesus. Finally, when He was about to go to Calvary, He said to His disciples, *"My time is at hand"* (Mt. 26:18). The dependent Man deliberately placed His times in God's hand.

After His brothers had gone to the feast a short while later, He remained in Galilee and waited there. He trusted in His Father's guidance and rested in Him. When His time finally came, He too went up to the feast—not publicly, but *"in private"* (John 7:10). He didn't let His brothers dictate to Him either the 'when' or the 'how,' but made both dependent on the guidance of God.

Incidentally, it's very encouraging to see that after Jesus' ascension, His brothers were among the believers who prayed together in the upper room and waited for the coming of the Holy Spirit. At least one of them, James, was even used to write a New Testament letter.[25] This should encourage us to continue praying for (yet) unbelieving relatives and to be a clear signpost pointing to Christ for them through our lives!

David is the man of whom we read most often in the Word of God that he asked the LORD. In 2 Samuel 5:18 we read, *"The Philistines had come and spread out in the Valley of Rephaim."* Faced with this danger, David asks the LORD whether he should go up against the enemies. The LORD answers and gives him the promise to deliver the

---

25 It could well be that the writer of the Epistle of Jude was also a brother of the Lord Jesus. He does not call himself a brother, but *"a servant of Jesus Christ,"* but he could also have done so out of reverence for his Lord. In any case it is striking that he calls himself brother of James, which very probably refers to the biological brother of Jesus and the writer of the Epistle of James.

Philistines into his hand. David acts in dependence on God, goes into battle and wins. Only four verses later it says, *"And the Philistines came up yet again and spread out in the Valley of Rephaim."* Suddenly David finds himself in an almost identical situation as shortly before. Under these circumstances, how many would simply have acted the same way as before, without asking God again! Why not just do exactly what worked well in the past? But instead of following pragmatic reasoning, the man according to God's heart remains dependent, even in this situation. Once again he turns to prayer and asks God for His will. Interestingly enough, the LORD tells him this time that now he should proceed differently. Again David wins— because he had consulted the LORD! How important it is that we are not pragmatic in our service to the Lord, but dependent on Him!

God always knows the right time for everything (see 1 Pet. 5:6). When we come before the throne of grace, He gives us grace and mercy to help us at the right time (see Heb. 4:16). Isaiah writes, *"Blessed are all those who wait for him"* (Isa. 30:18).

> *What can you learn from the behavior of David for your life of faith? For Elijah there was a time of seclusion and a time of public appearance (see 1 Ki. 17:3; 18:1). Do you also know such phases from your own experience? God's help never comes too late!*

Notes:

....

....

....

....

....

....

....

....

....

....

....

....

....

....

....

....

....

....

Dependence and the Glory of God

"When he heard that Lazarus was ill, he stayed two days longer in the place where he was." (John 11:6)

It must have been a great encouragement and comfort for the Lord Jesus to have a family at Bethany who valued Him and welcomed Him into their home. God blessed the devotion and obedience of these believers by giving them an awareness of Jesus' love (see John 14:21). When Lazarus became ill one day, his sisters sent a message to the Son of God, *"Lord, behold, he whom you love is ill"* (John 11:3).

But the fact that the Lord loves us doesn't save us from suffering. On the contrary, the Lord often uses needs and difficulties in our lives to make us grow in the awareness of His love and get to know Him better. This was also the case here. We can be sure that the two sisters never forgot Jesus' compassion and the tears He shed at their brother's grave for the rest of their lives! How true in this context are the words of Solomon, who says, *"There is a friend [a lover] who sticks closer than a brother"* (Prov. 18:24).

After the statement, *"Jesus loved Martha and her sister and Lazarus."* (John 11:5), we would have expected the Lord to set out as quickly as possible to meet this need. But that is exactly what He did not do. Instead, He patiently waited for God's timing—although Lazarus's health probably deteriorated hour by hour. The Lord had complete confidence that the Father had allowed this illness to happen in order to show His glory, and that He, the Son of God, would be glorified by it. Isaiah writes, *"Whoever believes will not be in haste [shall not hasten with fear]"* (Isa. 28:16). And so the Lord waited two full days before He set out on His journey. He didn't let Himself be guided by natural affections, but only by the will of God.

It requires faith to remain dependent and to wait for God in situations where the pressure is constantly increasing. Elijah stayed by the brook Cherith until the word of the LORD came to him—although the stream continued to dry up day after day. It's precisely in such circumstances that the Lord encourages us with the words, *"Did I not tell you that if you believed you would see the glory of God?"* (John 11:40).

> *How do you behave when you are waiting for guidance from the Lord, while humanly speaking, the pressure to act is continually increasing? Have you had periods of suffering in your life that you wouldn't have wanted to miss because you grew to know your Lord better?*
> *"We know that for those who love God all things work together for good"*
> *(Rom. 8:28).*

Notes:

A Path That a Bird of Prey Doesn't Know

"I will instruct you and teach you in the way you should go; I will counsel you with my eye upon you." (Psalm 32:8)

The Son of God experienced much resistance in Judea. The Jews there had often tried to lay hands on Him and kill Him (see John 7:1, 30, 44; 10:33). But this didn't prevent the Father from sending Him to this very region again. After the Lord had waited patiently for two days, God's time now arrived for Him: He must depart to raise Lazarus from the dead. So He said to His disciples, *"Let us go to Judea again"* (John 11:7).

It's interesting to see how the disciples reacted to the words of their Master: *"Rabbi, the Jews were just now seeking to stone you, and are you going there again?"* (John 11:8). Jesus' dependent and obedient act is immediately followed by indignation and incomprehension. How often we see the same pattern in our day.

If you live consistently in dependence on God, there will be people around you who won't understand you—especially when God sends you on a difficult or even dangerous mission. This is understandable, because others don't have the same exercise as you and have not experienced God's guidance in the decisions you are making. If purely rational reasons are given to dissuade you from a decision that you have made in dependence on your

Lord, then the following applies: *"Trust in the* LORD *with all your heart, and do not lean on your own understanding. In all your ways acknowledge him, and he will make straight your paths"* (Proverbs 3:5–6)!

Jesus' reaction to the disciples' objection is very instructive for us: *"Are there not twelve hours in the day? If anyone walks in the day, he does not stumble, because he sees the light of this world. But if anyone walks in the night, he stumbles, because the light is not in him"* (John 11:9–10). Because He walked in the light of the divine will, He could confidently leave the consequences of His actions to God. In this He fulfilled the words of the Psalmist: *"Your word is a lamp to my feet and a light to my path"* (Ps. 119:105).

When we make our decisions according to the Word of God, we walk in the light of God and can confidently place everything that worries us in His hands. Charles Stanley aptly said, "Obey God and leave all the consequences to Him." If you live in dependence on the will of God, you are immortal until your task here is fulfilled! The path of dependence is the path of blessing. *"That path no bird of prey knows, and the falcon's eye has not seen it. The proud beasts have not trodden it; the lion has not passed over it"* (Job 28:7–8).

> *Are you more likely to be guided by your natural mind or by the living Word and the Spirit of God? Are you willing to make yourself available to God for tasks that are difficult and dangerous?*
> *If the Lord has called you to a special task, do not be put off.*
> *God says, "My presence will go with you, and I will give you rest" (Ex. 33:14)!*

Notes:

....
....
....
....
....
....
....
....
....
....
....
....
....
....
....

The Unity of the Son with the Father Lived out in Practice

"As the living Father sent me, and I live because of the Father, so whoever feeds on me, he also will live because of me." (John 6:57)

In the life of Jesus the living Father was His starting-point, His motivation and His goal. He was one with the Father and yet at the same time dependent on Him in His thinking, in His words and in His deeds. He lived for the Father's sake and by every word that came out of His mouth (see Mt. 4:4).

This unity and dependence between the Father and the Son was evident in both what the Son spoke and what He did. Both are particularly evident in the Gospel of John.

Every time the Lord Jesus said something, He spoke in agreement with the Father. He did nothing of Himself, but spoke *"just as the Father taught me"* (John 8:28). It was the Father Who told Him what He should speak (see Isa. 50:4; John 12:49). Also, the teaching He brought didn't come from Him, but from the One Who sent Him (see John 7:16). In everything He represented the interests of His Father. This went even to the extent that, with full conviction, His Father's thoughts, goals and motives were His own.

Also in what He did, the Son was in perfect accord with His Father and always acted in dependence on Him. After He healed the lame man at the pool of Bethesda on the Sabbath, He told the Jews who accused Him, *"The Son can do nothing of himself save whatever he sees the Father doing: for whatever things he does, these things also the Son does in like manner"* (John 5:19). He was one with the Father in what He did, how He did it and when He did it.

As someone once aptly said, "The Father showed the Son all that He Himself did, and that is what the Son did, and nothing else (see John 8:29). This unity in action ultimately leads to the statement: *"the Father who dwells in me does **his** works"* (John 14:10). Father and Son are so in agreement that the works that are seen in the Son can ultimately be attributed to the Father." Therefore He also said, *"Whoever has seen me has seen the Father"* (John 14:9) and *"I and the Father are one."* (John 10:30).

Only when we prayerfully study the life of the Son of God, 'eating' Him in this way and appropriating Him, are we able also to live by Him (see John 6:57). It is inconceivable that a Christian could live a healthy spiritual life without daily nourishment from the manna (the life of Jesus as man on earth) or the produce (or: old corn) of the land (Christ in glory).

> *What does it mean practically for you to live for Jesus' sake? How much time and energy do you spend 'appropriating' the life of your Lord? Become newly aware of what a privilege it is to live in fellowship and harmony with your Creator and Savior!*

Notes:

....

....

....

....

....

....

....

....

....

....

....

....

....

....

....

....

....

Fruit for Eternity

"Abide in me, and I in you. As the branch cannot bear fruit by itself, unless it abides in the vine, neither can you, unless you abide in me. I am the vine; you are the branches. Whoever abides in me and I in him, he it is that bears much fruit, for apart from me you can do nothing." (John 15:4–5)

The Lord Jesus often spoke of the fact that He could do nothing by Himself (see John 5:19, 30) and that it was the Father Who worked through Him. He abode in the love of His Father and His Father abode in Him—this was His source of joy (see John 14:10; 15:10–11). Now that He was about to leave this world, He challenged His disciples to remain in Him, the true Vine. These words were of the greatest importance to them. Why? Because, separated from Him, they could not have borne fruit that would have had eternal value!

As disciples of Jesus who want to learn from their Lord and Master, we should ask ourselves the following question: How did the Lord Jesus bear fruit for God here on earth? The answer is, by revealing the Father, living in dependence on Him, and making the fruit of the Spirit visible in Himself. He walked through the day with a continual attitude of prayer, being constantly led by the Holy Spirit and paying careful attention to every word that came out of the mouth of God. Everything He did found its origin in the living fellowship that He maintained with His Father at all times. This is our example to follow!

A disciple should on the one hand learn from his Master and on the other hand remain in Him, the true Vine—because the way of discipleship is also the way of dependence! But what does remaining in Him mean practically for us? It means that we don't let the connection to Him break, but rather involve Him in all situations of life, keep Him before us in thought and thus live in vital fellowship with Him (see Ps. 16:8). This also means that we must rely on Him in faith, as our inexhaustible source of help, expecting everything from Him and acting in dependence on Him. Whoever is thus *"in the shadow of the Almighty"* (Ps. 91:1) can say with conviction and confidence: *"All my springs are in you"* (Ps. 87:7)!

This is the fruit that the vine grower is looking for: the characteristics of the life of the Lord Jesus, such as His love, gentleness, humility, patience, zeal and obedience. We need not think of great tasks that impress people. Rather, it is about Christ being manifest in us (see Gal. 4:19) and thereby making visible the fruit of the Spirit as we faithfully carry out our daily duties, whether at home or at work, in private or in public. God is glorified when Christ lives in us, making His life visible in us (see Gal. 2:20; 2 Cor. 4:10).

> *How do you practically realize Jesus' command, "abide in me" (John 15:4)? Isn't it wonderful that His "divine power has granted to us all things that pertain to life and godliness" (2 Pet. 1:3)? Take the time to reflect on your life in the light of eternity and consider what really matters in the short time you have left on this earth!*

Notes:

....

....

....

....

....

....

....

....

....

....

....

....

....

....

....

Planted by Brooks of Water

"I chose you and appointed you that you should go and bear fruit and that your fruit should abide." (John 15:16)

The Lord Jesus is the true Joseph: a fruitful bough by a spring (Gen. 49:22). He trusted God and made Him the essence of His trust. Therefore, the word of Jeremiah also applies to Him, who says, *"He is like a tree planted by water, that sends out its roots by the stream, and does not fear when heat comes, for its leaves remain green, and is not anxious in the year of drought, for it does not cease to bear fruit."* (Jer. 17:8).

God's river is still full of water today (see Ps. 65:9). He is and remains *"the fountain of living water"* (Jer. 17:13), which meets the believer's every need. Everything we need to bear fruit we find in Him. But streams of living water can only flow from those who really come to the fountain and drink there (see John 7:37–38). God is the Source for the one who calls (see Jud. 15:19), Who revives all who come to the throne of grace with boldness.

Paul was someone who did just that. He lived according to the grace that his Lord had provided for him daily (see 2 Cor. 12:9–10). Whether he was going through ups or downs, abundance or deprivation, he was able to do it all through Christ, Who strengthened him (see Phil. 4:13). In spite of fear, persecution and famine, this man of God was completely convinced that his heavenly Master enabled him to be more than a conqueror (see Rom. 8:35–37). At a time when everyone abandoned him, he experienced the Lord's help and strength (see 2 Tim. 4:17). Confidence in the goodness of his Lord even gave the Apostle the boldness to write to the Romans, *"I know that when I come to you I will come in the fullness of the blessing of Christ"* (Rom. 15:29).

Hudson Taylor once aptly said, "Do not come and take a hasty sip; no, do not come and let your thirst be quenched, even for a short time. No! Drink or be drinking, constantly, habitually. The cause of the thirst may be incurable. A coming and a drinking may be refreshing and invigorating. But we should always come, always drink, without fear of ever emptying the spring or exhausting the stream!"[26]

"All my springs are in you."
(Psalm 87:7)

---

26 Howard and Geraldine Taylor (2009), *Hudson Taylor's Spiritual Secret*, Moody Publishers

How can you drink from the river of God today and experience that He is still the fountain for the one who calls? What is the best prerequisite for God to make you a channel of blessing, as Isaiah describes it, "The LORD will guide you continually and satisfy your desire in scorched places and make your bones strong; and you shall be like a watered garden, like a spring of water, whose waters do not fail" (Isa. 58:11)?

Notes:

....
....
....
....
....
....
....
....
....
....
....
....
....

Grace Triumphs

"Not I, but the grace of God that is with me." (1 Corinthians 15:10)

God doesn't give us strength and grace in advance, but only as we need it at that moment. Why does He do this? To keep us dependent on Him! The disciples who followed the Lord when He was here on earth were dependent on His grace every day. They received from Him *"grace upon grace"* (John 1:16)—that is, one grace replaced another. This is also true for us today, *"as your days, so shall your strength be"* (Deut. 33:25).

If we abide in the true Vine through living dependence, we will experience how He always has what we need ready for us. To remain in Him also means to take what He wants to give us. Paul writes to the Ephesians, *"Be strong in the Lord and in the strength of his might"* (Eph. 6:10). The same Apostle urges Timothy, *"You then, my child, be strengthened by the grace that is in Christ Jesus"* (2 Tim. 2:1).

The grace that was apparent in the Lord Jesus is the motivation for true discipleship. The deeper our awareness of this grace and our trust in it, the more we will put our lives in God's hands and desire to live in dependence on Him. This is a growth process. This is why Peter calls believers to grow in grace (see 2 Pet. 3:18). In the book of Ezekiel we find this truth beautifully illustrated in connection with the "river of grace" that flows out of the temple (see Ezekiel 47:3–6).

On our conversion we came into contact with the river of God's grace for the first time. As Paul writes, *"By grace you have been saved"* (Eph. 2:8). A child of God who stands in grace (see 1 Pet. 5:12) experiences how the grace of God carries us along the path of faith. The Israelites also experienced in type that their feet did not swell despite 40 years of traveling in the desert (see Deut. 8:4). God carries us through—water up to the ankles.

But if we follow the Lord resolutely, we too must reckon with suffering and persecution (see John 15:20). Sometimes it happens that we are afraid, we become tired and have trembling knees (see Isa. 35:3). It is precisely at such times that we have access to the throne of grace, where God wants to give us *"grace to help in time of need"* (Heb. 4:16)—water up to the knees.

If we want to serve the Lord, our self-confidence must be broken. Jacob only became "Israel"—a "wrestler of God"—after God dislocated his hip (an image of natural power). Even Paul was in danger of becoming proud and therefore useless in serving the Lord. That's why God provided a thorn in the flesh" (see 2 Cor. 12:7) for the Apostle so that His servant would learn to rely entirely on His grace. In this way he experienced God's power triumphing over his weakness. We too can have this experience—water up to the waist.

But growth in grace goes even further: God wants us to give up the wheel completely and throw ourselves wholeheartedly on Him in faith, the *"God of all grace"* (1 Pet. 5:10). To have no more ground under our feet means to be completely dependent on grace—water to swim in.

> *Are you ready to learn to no longer stand on your own feet, but to be really carried completely by grace and to 'swim' in it? That is the goal of God's ways with us! This means in a practical way that the stream sets the direction and no longer you yourself. But this can only become a reality if you follow your Lord in total surrender and give up your own life. Are you prepared to go that far?*

Notes:

....

....

....

....

....

....

Closing Thoughts

Our great God wants to use each of us to bear fruit that will last for eternity! In His Word, He has given us clear indications that show us how we can do this. In order to be a useful vessel in the hand of the Master, we should make ourselves totally available to Him daily and live in conscious dependence on Him!

Every day He has a specific will for us and the desire that we fulfill the tasks He has planned for us (see Eph. 2:10). If we lead a dedicated prayer life, make ourselves dependent on the guidance and power of the Holy Spirit and let the living Word of God speak to us, we will realize *"what is the will of God, what is good and acceptable and perfect"* (Rom. 12:2).

The life of intimate fellowship with the living God and doing His will gives true fulfillment and deep satisfaction—things the world doesn't know. Our Lord and Master exemplified this to us and said, *"I have set the LORD always before me; because he is at my right hand, I shall not be shaken. Therefore my heart is glad, and my whole being rejoices"* (Ps. 16:8–9). What a wonderful role model!

"It is enough for the disciple to be like his teacher, and the servant like his master" (Mt. 10:25). True discipleship consists in learning from the Master and becoming more like

Him. He longs for us to depend on Him every day in order to *"walk in the same way in which he walked"* (1 John 2:6).

A life in dependence on God is not a legal obligation. It is a response to the grace that the *"God of all grace"* (1 Pet. 5:10) has given us and gives us anew every day. The more we look at the Son of God, have Him before our eyes and grow in the awareness of God's grace, the more we will trust Him and will consequently also hand over the steering wheel of our lives to Him. We honor God when we 'let go' more and trust Him without hesitation!

"Blessed is the man who trusts in the LORD, whose trust is the LORD." (Jer. 17:7)

"Looking to Jesus,

the founder and perfecter of our faith"

(Hebrews 12:2)

Notes:

....
....
....
....
....
....
....
....
....
....
....
....
....
....
....
....
....
....
....
....
....
....
....
....
....
....
....
....
....

Notes: